THE SCIENCE OF
PHILIP PULLMAN'S
HIS DARK
MATERIALS

His Dark Materials
by Philip Pullman

The Golden Compass
The Subtle Knife
The Amber Spyglass

Lyra's Oxford

THE SCIENCE OF
PHILIP PULLMAN'S
HIS DARK MATERIALS

MARY AND JOHN GRIBBIN
WITH AN INTRODUCTION BY PHILIP PULLMAN

LAUREL-LEAF BOOKS

**Thanks to Philip Pullman for permission
to quote from His Dark Materials.**

Published by Laurel-Leaf
an imprint of Random House Children's Books
a division of Random House, Inc.
New York

Originally published in Great Britain by Hodder Children's
Books in 2003.

Published in hardcover in the United States by Alfred A. Knopf
Books for Young Readers, New York, in 2005. This edition
published by arrangement with Alfred A. Knopf
Books for Young Readers.

Laurel-Leaf and colophon are registered trademarks
of Random House, Inc.

www.randomhouse.com/teens

Educators and librarians, for a variety of teaching tools,
visit us at www.randomhouse.com/teachers

RL: 5.1
ISBN: 978-0-375-83146-1
July 2007
Printed in the United States of America
10 9 8 7 6 5 4 3 2
First Laurel-Leaf Edition

"When a distinguished but elderly scientist states that something is possible, he is almost certainly right. When he states that something is impossible, he is very probably wrong."

ARTHUR C. CLARKE

"I'll be looking for you, Will, every moment, every single moment. And when we do find each other again, we'll cling together so tight that nothing and no one'll ever tear us apart. Every atom of me and every atom of you...

We'll live in birds and flowers and dragonflies and pine trees and in clouds and in those little specks of light you see floating in sunbeams.... And when they use our atoms to make new lives, they won't just be able to take one, they'll have to take two, one of you and one of me, we'll be joined so tight...."

CONTENTS

✦

Science:
A very short
introduction

by Philip Pullman

Science was one of those things (music was another) that I was fascinated by at home and turned off by at school. Like many children who grew up in the 1950s, I read that great comic the *Eagle* every week, with the adventures of Dan Dare and his enemy, the Mekon; and one of the items I most enjoyed was the science feature, the explanation of such things as radar, or nuclear fission, or rocket propulsion. There was a comic-strip character called "Professor Brittain," a genial sort of boffin, as they used to call scientists, who explained it to a suitably wide-eyed boy and girl. I soaked it all up greedily.

Then there were our trips to the Science Museum in South Kensington. What a wonderful place that was, and still is! Photoelectric cells and calculating machines, pulleys and radio valves—I didn't understand much of it, but I loved it all. It meant excitement and wonder and amazement; it meant the sense that anything was possible, and that the Universe was huge and full of exciting things to discover.

So why didn't I like science at school?

One reason might be that although I'm a science

fan, I'm not fundamentally a scientist. I'm a story-teller. A genuine scientist would love the subject for itself; I think I love science for the stories that are told about it. I can't do the hard stuff, mathematics is a horrible struggle, but let Professor Brittain begin to explain gravity or nuclear radiation or how the Solar System was formed, and I'm spellbound.

I think there are many people like me, who love hearing about something we can't ourselves do. Those of us who enjoy reading about science are living in a lucky time. There has been a great wave of very good writing about science in recent years; it's easy now to find books on geology, or evolution, or physics, or genetic engineering, or all sorts of other sciences, which are brilliantly written and as exciting as any thriller.

And among the very best of the modern writers on science are Mary and John Gribbin. I've read many of their books; I've heard John lecture; I've learned an enormous amount from them. When I heard that they were interested in writing a book about the science of *His Dark Materials*, I felt as privileged as if Dan Dare had invited me for a flight in his rocket.

But I wondered what they'd find to say... because I wasn't writing about science, after all. I was writing about Lyra, and Will, and Mrs. Coulter and Lee Scoresby and Mary Malone and all the other characters; and although I did try to get a bit of science in, and to get it right, it was very much there as a background, as a sort of stage set for the story to take place in front of.

Take the idea of parallel worlds. Many writers have used this idea, though it doesn't always come with a scientific explanation. Lewis Carroll's Alice books both begin with Alice leaving her world—our world—and going to another, and *The Lion, the Witch and the Wardrobe* works in exactly the same way. So I wasn't being very original in using the basic idea.

What I did try to do was get the science right—though not for a scientific purpose: for a storytelling purpose. In my story, Lyra first becomes aware of the existence of other worlds when the witch's dæmon tells her about them. What I was trying to do in that passage was not so much explain that other worlds exist—I was trying to convey to the reader the sense of awe and mystery that suddenly comes over Lyra. And when Will, in *The Subtle Knife*, goes through the mysterious window under the hornbeam trees to enter the city of Cittàgazze, what I wanted the reader to feel was not a logical conviction but a sense of wonder. The purpose is different, you see.

But I did try to get it right. In the case of parallel worlds, I read as much as I could find about the matter; I went to a lecture by David Deutsch, a scientist who has done a great deal of research into the subject; and although I didn't understand very much, I hope I managed to absorb enough of the arguments to make the reader feel that the background was solid enough not to fall over when anyone leaned against it. I think if you're convinced by one part of the story, you're a little more willing to believe the rest of it. I don't mean believe it's true, of course; we know it's not true. I mean believe that it works. My test was always: "I don't know very much about this, but I do know something, and if I read this in a novel, would it make me think that the writer knew at least as much as I did and wasn't a complete fool?"

Introduction

Well, many people much more scientifically learned than I am have read this trilogy and found not too much, I hope, to quarrel with. Among them are the Gribbins, and the result of their reading is this book. When I first read it, I was enormously impressed by how clever I was. Then I read it again and realized that if I'd got anything scientific right in the first place, it was because of the work of writers like them, who had explained these difficult ideas—and many others—with such clarity and skill.

Real scientists and science fans alike will find all kinds of things here to delight them. And if my story has been the cause of it, then no one will be more delighted than me.

Philip Pullman

CHAPTER ONE

BRIGHT MATERIALS

The secret of science, and
all the stars that shine

"She walks in beauty, like the night
Of cloudless climes and starry skies;
And all that's best of dark and bright
Meet in her aspect and her eyes:
Thus mellowed to that tender light
Which heaven to gaudy day denies."

LORD BYRON

...her knowledge was patchy. She knew about atoms and elementary particles, and anbaromagnetic charges and the four fundamental forces and other bits and pieces of experimental theology, but nothing about the solar system. In fact, when Mrs. Coulter realized this and explained how the earth and the other five planets revolved around the sun, Lyra laughed loudly at the joke.

However, she was keen to show that she did know some things, and when Mrs. Coulter was telling her about electrons, she said expertly, "Yes, they're negatively charged particles. Sort of like Dust, except that Dust isn't charged."

Science is explainable magic. If you were a time traveler visiting our world from the ancient past, you would think that magic was everywhere around you. Planes flying, cars moving, even frozen food would seem strange and miraculous. They are not strange magic to us because we are used to them and because we know they work by science, not magic. In ancient times, people were amazed and awed by things like rainbows and eclipses, things they had no control over. We still can't control these things, but we aren't scared of them, because we understand the science behind them.

In Philip Pullman's *His Dark Materials* trilogy, when Lyra visits Will's world, things like cars seem magical to her. And in Lyra's world there are things, like the alethiometer, and Dust, that seem like magic to Will. But even these things are really based on science. We are going to tell you about that science, the science of *His Dark Materials*. The story is all about uncovering hidden truth. The truly big magic that Philip Pullman weaves into his story is the magic that understanding things and knowing how the world works makes it less scary. He shows us that knowledge and science put you more in control of things.

This means more than understanding how a frozen pizza is made. Understanding frozen pizza is pretty smart, but the understanding behind *His Dark Materials* involves the whole Universe. That's where the "Dark Materials" come from. We're not talking here about the kind of material used to make a shirt or a curtain, but much more mysterious stuff, a kind of invisible matter that fills the Universe.

The worlds inhabited by Lyra, Will, and the other characters are embedded in a sea of Dust, which falls on them from space, and is real, but cannot be seen by human eyes. The characters, especially Lyra and Will, are also surrounded by a sea of knowledge. There is information about the world that they know nothing about when the story begins, but that they learn about, with the help of the alethiometer, as their adventure unfolds.

Both these images are true. Knowledge really does make the world a better place to live in. And astronomers really do have evidence that there is about ten times as much dark stuff in our Universe as there are bright stars and galaxies. Just like Dust, this dark material is not like anything ever detected on Earth. It isn't made of the kind of atoms and molecules your body is made of, or the air you breathe, or anything you have ever touched or seen. But, like Lyra, we have to know about things like atoms and electrons before we can learn about the dark materials in the Universe. And, unlike Lyra, we know a great deal about what goes on in space—not just in our Solar System, where there are actually nine planets, not six, but in the stars and galaxies beyond the planets.

THE STUFF OF THE UNIVERSE

What are atoms? Atoms are tiny particles that move around all the time, bouncing off one another and sometimes sticking together to make molecules. The discovery of atoms is the most important discovery in the whole of science. There are approximately two and a half centimeters in one inch, and an atom is only about one hundred-millionth of a centimeter across, so it would take ten million atoms side by side to stretch across the gap between two of the "teeth" on the jagged edge of a postage stamp. The oxygen molecules that you breathe in to stay alive are made of two oxygen atoms joined together. They don't just waft around gently in the air waiting for you to come along and breathe them in. When it comes to speed, they can go 50 times faster than the fastest 100-yard sprinter, and they never stop for a rest.

Oxygen molecules in the air move at about one-third of a mile per second. If they went in a straight line, they could cover more than 18 miles in a minute. But they never get a chance to go far, because they are always bouncing off other molecules in the air. The average distance they travel between collisions is just five millionths of an inch. They are so close together that they collide with other molecules three and a half billion times every second. That makes 210 billion collisions every minute. Feel free to work out how many that is in a day, a week, a century....

Atoms come in different varieties, corresponding to different kinds of material called elements. There are 92 different elements (things like oxygen, gold, or the silicon used in computer chips) that occur naturally on Earth. Because each variety of element corresponds to a different variety of atom, this means there are 92 different kinds of atoms. Everything we experience in our everyday lives is thanks to these 92 kinds of atoms interacting with each other in different ways. All the stuff around you, everywhere in the Universe, that is made of atoms is called baryonic matter.

THE LIGHT THAT SHINES

When atoms get hot, they radiate energy in the form of light—they shine. The white light that surrounds you in daylight is made of all the colors of the rainbow mixed together. In a rainbow, the colors are spread out to make a spectrum. You can do the same thing by shining light through a triangle of glass, called a prism, to make a spectrum. If you hang a prism in a window on a sunny day, it makes rainbow patterns that dance on the walls. The rainbow pattern is made because the light gets bent when it goes through the prism. Different colors are bent by slightly different amounts, so the colors get spread out. The same thing happens in raindrops to make rainbows. Raindrops are like tiny prisms.

One of the great discoveries of science in the nineteenth century was that each kind of atom shines in a particular way, making its own contribution to the rainbow spectrum of light. This role of the atom is an example of a hidden truth.

All the colors of the rainbow are made by light from shining atoms. Sodium atoms shine very brightly with yellow light. Sodium atoms in the gas in streetlights get their energy from electricity and turn it into yellow light. Every time you see that sort of yellow light, you know sodium is there, even if you can't touch it. If you ever see someone throw ordinary salt into a fire, you see a flash of the same "street lamp" yellow light. That is because salt molecules are made of sodium atoms joined to chlorine atoms (the chemical name for salt is sodium chloride).

BEYOND THE RAINBOW

On Earth, chemists can study the light from every kind of atom and measure the exact color it contributes to the spectrum. A little piece of magic turned into science. Astronomers can take this magic out into space. They measure the strength of light of different colors coming from the Sun and the stars, so they can work out what the stars are made of without ever going into space. That would have seemed like magic even a couple of hundred years ago. We actually know what the stars are made of, even though they are so far away that the light from them takes hundreds or thousands of years to get to us.

The scientific magic of the spectrum shows that all the stars—everything we can see in the Universe—are made of the same kind of atoms that we are made of. It is all baryonic matter.

STARS LIKE DUST

The Sun looks big and bright to us, and we see it in daylight, not at night. But it is an ordinary star. It is about 109 times bigger across than the Earth is and contains about 330,000 times as much material as the Earth does. It shines because, deep inside the Sun, one kind of atom (hydrogen) is being turned into another kind of atom (helium). This process is called nuclear fusion. When light atoms fuse together, they release energy. All stars shine in the same way.

The Sun looks very bright to us because it is quite close, in cosmic terms. The Earth orbits around the Sun once every year, at a distance of about 93 million miles. That's very nearly 400 times farther away from us than the Moon. But it's just next door in the Cosmos.

Other stars are just as bright as the Sun. Some of them are even brighter. But even extra-bright stars look faint to us because they are so far away. If you stood near a huge bonfire, it would look big and bright. But if you stood on a hill a few miles away and looked down on the bonfire, it would look like a tiny flickering flame. It's the same with stars, but the distances are much more than a few miles. Even stars that are quite close to us by cosmic standards are hundreds of thousands of times farther away than the Sun. And there are thousands and thousands of stars so far away that they are too faint to see at all without a telescope.

On a dark, moonless night, far from the city lights, you can see a white band of light across the sky. This is called the Milky Way. Telescopes show that the Milky Way is made up of millions and millions of stars, like a band of white dust scattered across the sky. The Sun is one of the stars of the Milky Way Galaxy. This Milky Way Galaxy is a disk of stars, shaped a bit like a huge fried egg, so big that it would take a beam of light 100,000 years to travel from one side to the other, even though light travels at 186,000 miles a second, or six trillion miles in a year. This huge distance is called a light-year. If you were as near to one of these stars as we are to the Sun, it would look as big and bright as the Sun. There are hundreds of billions of stars like the Sun in the Milky Way Galaxy.

Universes beyond the Universe

But this is not the end of the story. Until the 1920s, astronomers thought that the Milky Way Galaxy was the entire Universe, everything that there is. That's less than 100 years ago. Since then, bigger and better telescopes have made it possible to look farther and farther into the Cosmos. Astronomers found that there are other galaxies, like islands in the sea of space, beyond the Milky Way. In a way, they are like other universes. But they are not the kind of other universes that Philip Pullman writes about.

The light from these galaxies tells us that they are made of ordinary stars and ordinary atoms just like the ones on Earth and in the Sun. Our Milky Way is an average-sized galaxy. Beyond the Milky Way, the Cosmos contains hundreds of billions of galaxies, each containing hundreds of billions of stars. All this bright stuff, in every star in every galaxy, is baryonic matter—it is all made of atoms. Galaxies so far away that the light we see from them left their stars even before the time of the dinosaurs here on Earth are all made of baryonic matter, just like the matter you are made of and everything you touch is made of.

All this is our kind of magic; the scientific magic of the world we live in. Philip Pullman's "Dark Materials" might seem like a different kind of magic, pure fantasy that he has invented to make a good story. The amazing thing is, though, that these Dark Materials are also part of the scientific magic of our own world. This is such an amazing story that it deserves a chapter to itself.

CHAPTER TWO

DARK MATERIALS

THE HIDDEN WORLD, AND THE NATURE OF DUST

✦

"THERE ARE MORE THINGS IN HEAVEN AND
EARTH, HORATIO, THAN ARE DREAMT OF
IN YOUR PHILOSOPHY."

WILLIAM SHAKESPEARE

"Dark matter is what my research team is looking for. No one knows what it is. There's more stuff out there in the universe than we can see, that's the point. We can see the stars and the galaxies and the things that shine, but for it all to hang together and not fly apart, there needs to be a lot more of it— to make gravity work, you see. But no one can detect it. So there are lots of different research projects trying to find out what it is, and this is one of them."

As Mary Malone explains to Lyra, there's more to the Universe than meets the eye. At one level, the Dark Materials are Dust—something that can't be seen but is really there, in Lyra's world as well as in our own. But this is also a metaphor for another kind of dark material—hidden knowledge, and hidden forces, like Mrs. Coulter and the General Oblation Board carrying out their plans in secret. And even they don't know what is really going on at a deeper level still. It's like those sets of Russian dolls with one doll inside another, inside another, and so on, right down to a tiny little doll in the middle.

Our Universe is a bit like that. When astronomers started looking at the sky and studying stars and galaxies with their telescopes, they thought that all this bright stuff was all that really mattered. But in the second half of the twentieth century, less than 50 years ago, they found out that they were wrong. They found out that there is ten times more dark matter in the Universe than all the bright stuff put together.

It's like an iceberg. When you see an iceberg floating in the sea, it looks big and white and shiny. But there is actually ten times as much ice underneath the water, hidden in the dark, where you can't see it. This is the idea behind Dust—the Dark Materials of the story. But if you can't see the dark stuff, how do astronomers know that it is there?

STRETCHING LIGHT

When you know enough about astronomy, the light from other galaxies tells you more than just what those galaxies are made of. It can also tell you how they move. Astronomers use special detectors to measure light from distant galaxies, just as Lord Asriel uses special detectors to photograph Dust. If you don't know how they do it, the things they discover seem like magic. But it is real science.

If something is moving toward us, the whole spectrum of light from it gets squashed up. If something is moving away from us, the whole pattern gets stretched out. A bit like a Slinky—if you pull it, it gets longer, but if you push it, it gets squashed up.

The same thing happens with sound. When a fire engine is rushing toward you, the sound of its siren gets squashed up, and this squashing makes the note of the siren higher. When it is moving away, the sound gets stretched out, so the note is deeper. Anyone who knows this bit of scientific magic could measure how fast the fire engine is going by measuring how much the note changes as it goes past. Astronomers can use the same sort of trick to measure how fast galaxies are moving.

They can do this even if the galaxies are millions of light-years away from us. And it is this stretched starlight that tells us the Universe really is full of dark material.

COMING TO GRIPS WITH GRAVITY

Galaxies come in groups called clusters. They move about within the clusters, like bees buzzing about in a swarm. But all the clusters are moving away from one another, like lots of different swarms of bees spreading out in all directions. The whole big Universe is expanding. But if the clusters are getting farther and farther apart, that means that once upon a time they were closer together. If you are in a car moving north up the M1 motorway, a highway in England, you are getting farther and farther away from London. So you must have started out much closer to London. If there were a lot of cars all heading out away from London, in all different directions, it would mean they all started from London. If you knew how fast they were going, you could work out when they all started out.

In the same way, by measuring how quickly the clusters are moving apart, astronomers can work backward to figure out how long it has been since everything was piled up in one place. Everything we can see in the Expanding Universe today started spreading out from a single point of space and time just under 14 billion years ago. This is called the Big Bang. The kind of astronomers who study this are called cosmologists. It takes years of study to understand the Big Bang and the Expanding Universe—but, in spite of all this brainwork, most cosmologists are nowhere near as crazy as Jotham Santelia, the cosmologist who is imprisoned by the bear Iofur Raknison in *The Golden Compass*.

How do we know what it was like in the Big Bang in which the Universe was born? Cosmologists can work out what things were like in the Big Bang by imagining time running backward, so that all the galaxies and all the stars, and eventually all the atoms, move together until they are piled up in that single point of space and time. It's like running a video backward to find the beginning of a film. If the film showed a building being blown up by a demolition expert, the backward film would show all the bricks moving together to make a building.

In the Beginning

Cosmologists don't have a movie of the Big Bang. But they can work out what happened. They know what happened because physicists, people like Mary Malone, can make little bubbles of very hot energy by smashing beams of particles together in giant machines called accelerators. The particles travel at very nearly the speed of light and smash into each other head-on.

Two of the biggest accelerators in the world are at CERN, near Geneva, Switzerland, and at Fermilab, near Chicago. First, the physicists make the bubbles of energy in their accelerators; then, using very sensitive detectors, they watch how the energy turns into material particles. This is one of the most amazing discoveries in science. If you have pure energy—like sunlight, only much, much stronger—it can be turned into material particles. That's where the stuff we are made of came from. Cosmologists can actually work out how much baryonic matter, the kind of atoms that plants and planets and people are made of, was made in the Big Bang. And this turns out to be a clue to how much dark material there is in the Universe.

At the very beginning of time, nearly 14 billion years ago, the Universe was so hot that there were no atoms and molecules, just a fireball of pure heat energy. There was so much energy in the Big Bang that it could make enough material for all the stars and galaxies we can see, and a lot more besides.

STARDUST

The atoms that came out of the Big Bang were almost all hydrogen and helium. These are the two simplest elements. There wasn't time for anything more complicated to be made before the fireball cooled down. So the very first stars that were born were made of about 75 percent hydrogen and 25 percent helium. All the other elements, including the ones you are made of, were made inside stars by nuclear fusion. They were spread out through space when those stars died, and eventually went to make new stars, planets, and people. You are made of stardust.

But the Big Bang fireball could not have cooked up enough baryonic atoms to provide all of the dark material in the Universe today. Because astronomers can measure how fast galaxies are moving inside clusters, they know how much material must be in the clusters to hold them together by gravity. If there were not enough material in the Sun, its gravity would not be strong enough to stop the planets from flying off into space. If there were not enough material in Planet Earth, you would not be held down to the ground. If there were not enough material in a cluster, its gravity would not be strong enough to stop the galaxies from flying away into space. This is what Mary Malone is referring to when she tells Lyra about the way clusters of galaxies hang together without flying apart.

ΠOT STARS ALOΠE

How do we know how much material there is in all the stars of a galaxy? Because astronomers can measure the material's brightness. The brightness of a star like the Sun depends on how much material there is in it (its mass). The brighter a star, the more material it must contain.

From the brightness of a whole galaxy of stars, it is possible to work out how much material there is in all the bright stars put together. Astronomers can work this out for clusters of galaxies in the Expanding Universe as well. To explain the way galaxies move, you need about 50 times more material than all the bright stuff we can see in all the galaxies and clusters revealed by our best telescopes. You need Dust—or something very like Dust—as well as stardust.

This was a big surprise to scientists. It's as if you saw a soda can in the road and kicked it because you thought it was empty. If it was really full of fizzy soda, it would be much heavier than you expected. The kick would hurt your toe, and the can wouldn't move as fast as you thought it would. The Universe is like that. It is full of something we can't see. (Definitely not fizzy soda!)

But what about all the clouds of cold gas and dust between the stars? They don't shine, but they are made of baryonic atoms, and they tug on things by gravity. You might think these invisible clouds of cold baryons could explain how galaxies move. But there are not enough of them.

DARK STUFF

The Big Bang calculations tell us that there cannot be more than ten times as much baryonic material as there is in all the bright stars in all the galaxies put together. But we need 50 times as much to explain how galaxies move. So even adding the dark baryonic material in—all the atoms in the Universe—we still need five times more material to hold everything together. There must be at least five times as much extra material, not made of atoms at all, out there. It cannot be made of atoms, so it must be made of some sort of particles not yet detected on Earth. And it cannot shine, or we would see it. It is dark material.

Between 80 percent and 95 percent of the material of the Universe really is made of this stuff, which astronomers call non-baryonic Cold Dark Matter—or CDM, for short. This is the real science behind the Dark Materials in the trilogy.

WHERE IS DARK MATTER?

If these Cold Dark Matter particles are spread out evenly around our own Milky Way Galaxy, there would be one or two of them in every cubic inch of space. There would be about 100 Cold Dark Matter particles in every quart of everything. Not just every quart of "empty space" up above the atmosphere, but whizzing through the air that you breathe and every quart of liquid you drink, through your own body and through the solid Earth, without having any effect on the atoms at all. Or perhaps the particles in dark matter clump together to make tiny grains, like fine sand, or like the tiny particles of soot in cigarette smoke. If you could see them, these grains would look like dust.

FROM DUST TO DUST

Does that sound familiar? The only way these Cold Dark Matter particles affect atoms is by gravity, and the gravity of a single particle (or even a clump of them) is much too small to notice. But the gravity of the whole Earth is much too big not to have an effect on these particles, or grains of dust, which are bound to be tugged toward our planet. In *The Golden Compass*, on an expedition to the far north, Lord Asriel has taken a slide with a special photographic emulsion. The special emulsion is fiction, but we know many astronomers who would give almost anything to have a camera that could photograph what it "sees." Philip Pullman describes how Lord Asriel shows the slide to the scholars at Jordan College:

...it was as if the moonlight had been filtered out. The horizon was still visible, with the dark shape of the hut and its light snow-covered roof standing out, but the complexity of the instruments was hidden in darkness. But the man had altogether changed: he was bathed in light, and a fountain of glowing particles seemed to be streaming from his upraised hand.

"That light," said the Chaplain, "is it going up or coming down?"

"It's coming down," said Lord Asriel, "but it isn't light. It's Dust."

CHAPTER THREE

NORTHERN LIGHTS

LIGHTS IN THE SKY, AND
THE MAGNETIC WEB

◆

" Man is occupied and has been persistently
occupied since his separate evolution,
with three kinds of struggle: first with
the massive, unintelligent forces of nature,
heat and cold, winds, rivers, matter and energy;
secondly, with the things closer to him, animals
and plants, his own body, its health and disease;
and lastly, with his desires and fears,
his imaginations and stupidities."

J. D. Bernal

Her wonder was so strong that she had to clutch the rail to keep from falling.

The sight filled the northern sky; the immensity of it was scarcely conceivable. As if from Heaven itself, great curtains of delicate light hung and trembled. Pale green and rose-pink, and as transparent as the most fragile fabric, and at the bottom edge a profound and fiery crimson like the fires of Hell, they swung and shimmered loosely with more grace than the most skillful dancer.

✦

This is the first time Lyra sees the Northern Lights, from the ship that carried her and the Gyptians north to Lapland.

It's the same in our world. Anyone who has seen the Northern Lights will tell you that they are magical. The swirl of colored light across a dark sky is like a light show put on by the gods themselves. It's easy to see why these lights were woven into the stories told by Norsemen stunned by their power and mystery, and why they became part of the Viking sagas.

The scientific explanation of the Northern Lights shows us how something that used to be thought of as magic becomes science when you understand it. But that doesn't make it any less awesome. If you understand the science, the Northern Lights are even more amazing, and you can still enjoy the light show.

The Northern Lights are seen as colored patterns, like waterfalls and rivers of light, in the northern sky. They are visible from places like Canada, northern Scotland, and Norway. There have been rare sightings as far south as England, or even in the Mediterranean. The Northern Lights are also known as the Aurora Borealis; the same swirls of light are seen in the sky near the South Pole, but the lights appearing there are called the Aurora Australis. The auroras are often red, yellow, or green, and sometimes form shimmering arches of light in the sky. It's no wonder that the Vikings and other northern people in our world, just like the northern people in Lyra's world, thought that the arches might provide a bridge to another world.

THE MAGIC OF MAGNETISM

The science-that-used-to-be-magic involved with the Northern Lights is magnetism. People have known about magnetism for thousands of years. At first, it was thought of as a source of strong magic. The ancient Greeks who were around 3,000 years ago knew about natural magnets, lumps of magnetic rock called lodestone. But they didn't know how magnetism worked, and they believed wild stories about magnetic mountains in far-off lands, where the magnetism of the rocks was so strong that if you wore shoes with iron nails they would stick so hard to the ground that you wouldn't be able to lift your feet. People also believed that lodestones had magical powers to cure illnesses and thought that if you had a bad leg, you could make it better by putting a lodestone on it and wrapping it up tightly with a bandage. And they thought that a piece of lodestone would stop being magnetic if somebody with garlicky breath breathed on it.

Magnetism didn't start being scientific until a bit more than 400 years ago, at the end of the sixteenth century, when Queen Elizabeth I and William Shakespeare were alive. The person who made magnetism scientific was a doctor named William Gilbert. He was such a good doctor that eventually he became one of the physicians at the court of the queen.

Before he became a court physician, in the 1570s Gilbert was the first person to study magnetism scientifically. Actually, he was the first person to study *anything* scientifically. Before Gilbert came along, people had no explanation for how the world worked except for magic and the influence of the gods. They had no idea why planets orbit around the Sun (lots of people didn't even believe that planets did orbit the Sun), or why we have seasons instead of having the same weather all the time, or how people catch illnesses, or anything else.

So William Gilbert was the first scientist. What made him a scientist was that he didn't believe stories just because lots of people said they were true, but he carried out experiments to test them. For example, he rubbed magnets all over with garlic to see if that stopped them from being magnetic. It didn't. The story was just an old wives' tale. And he carried out lots of other experiments as well and wrote about them, in Latin, in a book called *De Magnete*. It was published in 1600, one year after Shakespeare's play *Julius Caesar* was performed in London for the first time. The kind of world Gilbert lived in, with its Oxford colleges, religion, and no cars or planes, was rather like Lyra's world in many ways.

The magnetic Earth

The most important thing Gilbert discovered was that the Earth itself is a magnet and that its magnetic influence extends out into space. Before he came along, people thought that magnetic compass needles pointed north because they were attracted by the North Star or because there was a great magnetic island somewhere near the North Pole. But Gilbert guessed that the Earth itself is a magnet. He tested his idea with experiments. He made spherical magnets, carved out of lodestone, to copy the shape of the Earth. They were models of the magnetic Earth.

Gilbert used a tiny compass needle to measure how the magnetic influence varied all over the surface of his models. One end of a compass needle (which is just a tiny magnet) points north, and the other end points south. You could put the pointer on either end. It's just a convention to say it points north. All the magnetic patterns Gilbert investigated showed up both for the magnetic spheres and for the real Earth. So the real Earth must be a magnetic sphere.

Since Gilbert's time, scientists have learned a lot more about the way the Earth's magnetic influence (which is usually called its magnetic field) extends out into space. We know this because we now have measurements from spacecraft and from all over the surface of the planet itself, not just the magnetic models. We think of the magnetic field as being made up of "lines of force" that stretch from the north magnetic pole to the south magnetic pole. Above the equator, these lines run parallel to each other, one on top of the other, making layers like an onion that has been sliced in half. They make a kind of magnetic shield, above the atmosphere but between the Earth and space. But at the magnetic poles, the lines of force bunch together and funnel down toward the ground, making two holes in this shield. It is these holes that are responsible for the Northern and Southern Lights.

The holes are only important because there is something in space that cannot cross magnetic lines of force, but can get into the holes. This isn't dark material—dark material isn't affected by magnetism at all. It is ordinary baryonic matter, but not quite in the form of the atoms that make up your body and the pages of this book.

Inside the Atom

Atoms are made up of even smaller pieces. These are called subatomic particles. Every atom has a nucleus at its center. The nucleus of an atom of the simplest element, hydrogen, is just a single particle, called a proton, which has a positive electric charge. This proton is accompanied by a single electron (which has a negative electric charge), which you can think of as orbiting around the nucleus.

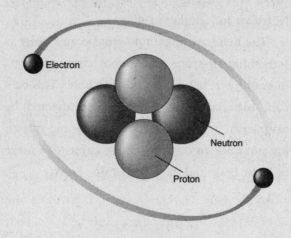

Helium atom (not to scale).

In all other atoms, the nucleus is made of a mixture of protons and particles called neutrons, which are similar to protons but have no electric charge. Protons and neutrons are each roughly 2,000 times heavier than electrons.

The number of protons tells you what element the atom is. Hydrogen has one proton, helium has two, oxygen has eight, and so on. And there is always the same number of electrons orbiting in the outer region of the atom as there are protons in the nucleus, so that the total electric charge on an atom is zero. The electrons and the protons cancel each other out.

But if an electron got loose from its atom, it would carry electricity with it. That's what's happening when electricity flows down wires. Millions and millions of electrons are moving along the wire. Electrically charged particles also interact with magnetic fields. They spiral tightly around magnetic field lines, moving along them like beads on a wire. Any electrically charged particles from space that come near the Earth can't get through the magnetic field above the equator;

they are trapped on the field lines and shunted toward the magnetic poles.

BEHIND THE NORTHERN LIGHTS

Electrically charged particles reach the Earth from space because atoms get knocked about in violent collisions, and some of the electrons are knocked away from the nucleus completely. The bit of atom left behind is called an ion. An ion has a positive charge (positive electricity) because some of the negative electricity has been taken away from it. In fact, the collisions don't necessarily have to be very violent—when you comb your hair on a dry day, you can rub away some of the electrons, making your hair positively charged (so it stands on end) and the comb negatively charged (so it picks up small pieces of paper). On a larger scale, collisions between hailstones inside storm clouds separate out the electric charge, which builds up until there is a flash of lightning to restore the balance. In a lightning flash, the negative electricity flows back to the positive electricity and cancels it out again.

Some particles from space come from really far away, farther than the Sun or planets. They may actually come from other stars and galaxies. But most of the space particles that reach the Earth come from the Sun.

The Sun is so hot that atoms inside it bash into each other hard enough to knock electrons free. Even on the outside, it is shining as hot as the glowing filament in an old-fashioned lightbulb. That's almost 11,000 degrees Fahrenheit. In the middle, the temperature soars to about 27 million degrees Fahrenheit.

Electrons and ions from the Sun stream out into space and past the Earth and the other planets like a wind, called the Solar Wind. The particles in the Solar Wind travel in space at about 310 miles per hour, until something gets in their way.

We cannot see the Solar Wind, but it can be detected and studied by spacecraft. And we can see what happens when the Solar Wind blows on the Earth. The Earth's magnetic field forms a shield around the Earth called the magnetosphere. This protects us from charged particles everywhere

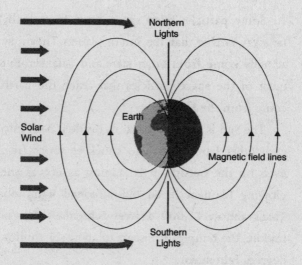

Earth's magnetosphere.

except at the poles. So the electrically charged particles from the Solar Wind are funneled down onto the poles of the Earth. They don't affect people because they never reach the ground. They give their energy to atoms high up in the atmosphere, and that is what makes the Northern Lights.

The atoms in the atmosphere that get energy from the Solar Wind are mostly nitrogen and oxygen. When the Solar Wind is blowing strongly, it heats up the top of the atmosphere to a temperature of more than 1,800 degrees Fahrenheit. This is like the way the electricity in streetlights gives its energy to sodium atoms in the gas inside the lights and makes them glow. Another place you see glowing atoms that have been excited by electricity is in neon signs. The Northern Lights are nature's neon signs.

Excited atoms

Atoms that have extra energy are said to be excited, and excited sodium atoms glow yellow. There are a few sodium atoms in the atmosphere, so there is a little bit of yellow in the Northern Lights. But when oxygen atoms are excited, they glow red and green, two colors seen very strongly in the auroras. The Northern Lights are caused by excited atoms in the atmosphere shining with their own characteristic colors of light, and the patterns shift as the Solar Wind blows about in gusts from one spot to another.

The lights are made high in the atmosphere,

between about 60 and 200 miles above the ground, on the edge of space where the air is far too thin to breathe. Even Mount Everest is just under six miles high, so the auroras are at least ten times higher above sea level than the tip of Mount Everest. The bottom of the Northern Lights is usually red, but from 60 miles up to about 155 miles they are mainly green, sometimes with white, yellow, or blue mixed in. The higher part of the aurora is usually red. Or as Lord Asriel describes the appearance of the aurora in one of his slides:

... *pale green and rose, for the most part, with a tinge of crimson along the lower edge of that curtain-like formation.*

Exploring the Sky

People have known about the Northern Lights for as long as they have been watching the northern skies, and the auroras were written about in ancient times by the Chinese, Greeks, Japanese, and Koreans. They were also described in religious chronicles from medieval times and in Viking tales from more than 1,000 years ago. The famous astronomer Edmond Halley, who gave his name to a comet, observed a great aurora from London in 1716, and Captain James Cook saw the Aurora Australis in 1773. But nobody had any idea what caused the lights until the end of the nineteenth century.

Nobody knew what made the Northern Lights shine before then because electrons and ions hadn't been discovered. Electrons were discovered in the 1890s, and right away the Norwegian scientist Kristian Birkeland realized that electrons from the Sun caused the Northern Lights. He made three expeditions to the far north and set up a laboratory at 70°N latitude to study the aurora. That's right at the frozen tip of northern Norway, farther north than Iceland (and he had to go in winter so he could see the Northern Lights properly).

Scientific explorers like Birkeland were just the same kind of tough people as Will's father, but not quite as rough and tough as Lee Scoresby, the aeronaut. They didn't have modern weatherproof clothing made of fabrics like nylon. They had to wear the same kind of clothes that Lyra is dressed up in when she has to travel to the same part of her world:

... a parka made of reindeer skin, because reindeer hair is hollow and insulates well; and the hood was lined with wolverine fur, because that sheds the ice that forms when you breathe.... Finally they bought a waterproof cape that enveloped her completely, made of semitransparent seal intestine.

STORMS FROM THE SKY

Less than 150 years ago, nobody knew about electrons. But our modern world runs almost entirely on electricity. For a start, where would we be without computers? Even modern cars have computers to make them work, and we are used to washing machines, electric light, electric trains, and many more things powered by electricity. Most of these things also have computers built into them. The electricity is generated in power stations and sent to where it is needed along power cables strung between tall towers. All this means that the Solar Wind can do much more to us today than put on a show of pretty lights.

When electrically charged particles disturb magnetic fields they make radio waves. This happens all the time when particles from the Sun interact with the Earth's magnetic field and spiral toward the poles. These radio waves can be picked up by suitable instruments. But sometimes there is a great outburst of activity on the Sun. This can send a huge blast of particles—a storm in the Solar Wind—toward us.

A Solar Storm like this can knock out satellites in space (including communications satellites and the satellites that beam TV pictures around the world) when the particles hit the sensitive electronic equipment in the satellites. When these particles hit the Earth's magnetic field, they produce a huge aurora, like the one seen by Halley in 1716. They also make a great blast of radio waves, called an electromagnetic pulse. Such a pulse didn't matter in Halley's time, because there was no electronic equipment then. But today it could fry the memory chips inside computers and produce a surge of electricity in power lines in northern countries such as Canada, blowing all the fuses and cutting off the electricity supply.

But don't panic. Even though storms in the Solar Wind may involve a billion tons of gas hurtling toward us at speeds of up to 1,300 miles per second, they have a long way to come. It takes almost a day for these storms from space to get from the Sun to the Earth. Astronomers can see storms brewing on the Sun with their telescopes, so we ought to get plenty of warning if something like this is on the way. The light carrying news of the coming storm travels at more than 186,000 miles per second, so it will reach us long before the particles do. As long as people in northern lands are aware of the danger, they can turn their computers and other electrical equipment off and wait for the storm to pass before turning them on again. We can hide our computers from the storm, just like the way people in some parts of the world shelter in storm cellars while a hurricane passes by.

The celestial fireworks of the Northern Lights are a sign of the way in which the entire Earth interacts with the Universe at large. The science behind them shows how we are under the influence of invisible forces that can change our lives. Lord Asriel knows this. He has to go to the far north to carry out his terrible experiments, because it is there that the shield of the Earth's magnetosphere is weakest, and he can tap into the energy of the Solar Wind to make a bridge between the worlds.

When the story starts, Lyra doesn't know any of this. But she soon learns where Lord Asriel is, and she knows she has to find him, because she has something more powerful than any electronic computer—the alethiometer, her golden compass.

CHAPTER FOUR

THE GOLDEN COMPASS

THE MEANING OF TRUTH, AND THE UNCONSCIOUS MIND

✦

"ANY SUFFICIENTLY ADVANCED TECHNOLOGY
IS INDISTINGUISHABLE FROM MAGIC."

ARTHUR C. CLARKE

The most magical thing in the whole *His Dark Materials* story is Lyra's alethiometer. The heavy instrument fits into the palm of her hand and looks:

...very like a clock, or a compass, for there were hands pointing to places around the dial, but instead of the hours or the points of the compass there were several little pictures, each of them painted with extraordinary precision, as if on ivory with the finest and slenderest sable brush.

Lyra thinks the alethiometer is made of brass and crystal, but the polished instrument gleams like gold. What does it do? It tells you the truth—if you know how to ask the right questions and how to interpret the answers. The name comes from *alétheia*, the Greek word for truth.

We all want to know the truth and to understand all that we are told, which is why the idea of the alethiometer is such a powerful one. People throughout history have longed to have something like this, which could tell them about the future and give them wise answers to their problems. Enigmatic oracles are traditional in stories of epic adventures, going right back to the legends of ancient Greece. The very name oracle comes from Greek stories, where people use oracles to ask questions of the gods. The replies they get can always be interpreted in at least two ways, and they are always true once you know which is the right interpretation.

But there's a catch. Oracles speak in mysteries. The person who interprets the oracle has to be clever enough to work out the message of truth and wisdom that the oracle is giving.

CONSULTING THE ORACLE

The Greeks, and people in other ancient cultures, really believed in oracles. There was a famous one at Delphi, in Greece. People would go to the priests or priestesses in charge of the oracle, make an offering to the gods, and ask their questions. The priests or priestesses would go away to "consult the oracle" and come back with an answer. Of course, the priests and priestesses were making up the answers themselves. That's why they were so careful to give ambiguous answers, so nobody could ever catch them in a mistake.

This is just like the way fortune-tellers still work today. You give them money (just like an offering to the gods) and they tell you things about your future that are vague enough that, whatever happens to you, you will think the "prediction" has come true. The trick is for them to be clever enough to find out things about you while talking to you and to weave these truthful things about you into the story. So if a fortune-teller noticed you had candy in your bag, she might tell you that you are probably going to get two cavities.

In the Sherlock Holmes stories, the famous detective is always amazing people by seeming to have strange psychic powers that reveal their secrets, then explaining how he worked it all out from a few simple observations.

CONSULTING THE SHERLOCK

In "The Adventure of the Blue Carbuncle," Sherlock Holmes hands a battered hat to his friend Dr. John Watson. Watson notices that it is a very ordinary hat, a bit the worse for wear, with a discolored red silk lining. The brim of the hat has holes for an elastic strap to secure it to the head, but the strap is missing. The hat is cracked, dusty, and spotted with blobs of wax and other marks that someone has tried to cover up with smears of ink.

Holmes then amazes his friend by telling him that the owner of the hat:

. . .was highly intellectual. . .that he was fairly well-to-do within the last three years, although he has now fallen upon evil days. He had foresight, but has less now than formerly, pointing to a moral retrogression, which, taken with the decline of his fortunes, seems to indicate some evil influence, probably drink, at work upon him. This may account also for the obvious fact that his wife has ceased to love him. . . .

He is a man who leads a sedentary life, goes out little, is out of training entirely, is middle-aged, has grizzled hair which he has had cut within the last few days, and which he anoints with lime-cream. . . .It is extremely improbable that he has gas laid on in his house.

When Holmes and Watson meet the owner of the hat, the description turns out to be exactly right! How did Sherlock the Oracle know? We won't tell you all his secrets, because we don't want to spoil the story for you if you want to read it yourself. For example, though, the foresight comes from the fact that the man had had an elastic strap fitted to the hat, but since he has lost the elastic and not bothered to replace it, he must have become more careless. And the blobs of wax are a sure sign that he lives in a house lit by candles, not by gaslight, which was the latest thing when the story was written.

It's obvious, once you know how to read the signs. But that's the trick—reading the signs.

THE SCIENCE OF TRUTH-TELLING

But Lyra's alethiometer is a machine. How could a machine do anything like that? The answer is that the machine isn't really doing it at all. Lyra is doing the truth-telling, with her own mind. The alethiometer gives her something to concentrate on while she is thinking. It also gives her the confidence to believe in her own deductions and to act on her own judgment. She has to ask her questions the right way, and that makes her think properly about the questions, so that her mind works out the answers unconsciously and the answers seem to pop into her head.

We can all do this a little bit. If you have a puzzle you can't solve, sometimes the best thing to do is try to forget about it, and even go to bed without working out the answer. The next day, you often find the answer has come into your mind. Your mind keeps working unconsciously even when you don't realize you are thinking about things.

But some people are much better at doing this. That's why Lyra can understand the alethiometer better than anyone else; she has the right kind of mind, a Sherlock Holmes sort of unconscious, for this kind of thinking. And when she gets older, she finds it harder and harder to understand the alethiometer, because the way her mind works is changing. In Pullman's story, adults can only understand the alethiometer if they look everything up in books, and it takes them hours, or days, to find the answers to questions, while Lyra can do it in a few minutes. The story is telling us that children are better at understanding new things, and imagining things, than adults are. Children's minds are always open to new ideas and imagination, but adults' minds are often bogged down by an inability to understand the unfamiliar. Even if that isn't true in our world (and perhaps it is!), it is certainly true in Lyra's world.

THE BOOK OF CHANGES

Even in our world, though, there is something that works like an alethiometer. It even has the books that tell you how to work out what the answers to your questions mean. This kind of oracle is called the I Ching, or the Book of Changes. It was developed in China in ancient times. Today, some people use the I Ching as a kind of game. You can "consult the oracle" at home, instead of traipsing all the way to Delphi. But some people still take it very seriously.

In the second volume of the trilogy, The Subtle Knife, the connection between the I Ching and the alethiometer's assistance is made plain. Lyra is searching for a scholar to help her, and with the alethiometer's assistance she finds Mary Malone, a scientist in our world who is investigating dark matter. It's Mary, by the way, who realizes that Lyra's alethiometer is made of gold, not brass. She has the symbols of the I Ching stuck up on the back of a door, as well as a computer with which she can communicate with the intelligence represented by Dust—what she calls Shadow Matter. The same talent that makes Lyra so good at understanding the alethiometer makes her good at communicating with the Shadows through the computer. The Shadows tell Lyra and Mary that when people use the I Ching, they are really talking to the Shadows.

So what is the I Ching? The symbols used in the I Ching are 64 hexagrams, each made up of six horizontal lines. Some of the lines are solid, and some have a gap in the middle. Each hexagram has a name, and each one is regarded as being made up of a pair of three-line symbols, called trigrams. Each trigram has its own meaning, and in the Book of Changes all these meanings are written down as commentaries.

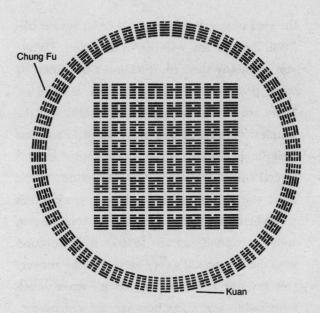

The 64 hexagrams of the I Ching, in the traditional
arrangement of a circle and a square.

CONSULTING THE I CHING

If you want to consult the I Ching, first of all you
have to think of the question you want to ask and
hold it firmly in your mind. It has to be a question about something you are planning to do, not

the kind of question with a yes or no answer like "Will the Red Sox win the World Series?" While you are doing this, you pick out a hexagram by some process that seems to work at random. There are several ways you can do this, but the simplest (explained in a book called I *Ching Coin Prediction*, by Da Liu) is to toss a set of three coins several times. Following the instructions in the book, the pattern of heads and tails you get tells you which hexagram to look at for your answer, and a second hexagram to take in connection with the first one. It's very easy—but the answers you get, the commentaries, don't make much sense unless you know how you are supposed to interpret them.

For example, hexagram number 20, called *Kuan*, looks like this:

and means "looking down." You might get it in conjunction with hexagram number 61:

which is Chung Fu, standing for "inward confidence and sincerity."

To find out what all this means, you have to look up the explanations in more books. They will tell you that "looking down" in this sense refers to people like kings and emperors, who look down on their subjects and transform them, and to wise people who understand the way the world works. "Inward confidence and sincerity" doesn't need much explanation, but the traditional interpretations stress that it is a sign of good fortune and success. Taken together, this is a very encouraging answer to whatever question might have been asked—the sort of combination

Lyra might have got if she had asked the I Ching whether to go on her quest.

GOOD NEWS AND BAD NEWS

But don't run away with the idea that, like many fortune-tellers, the I Ching provides only good news. Hexagram number 12, for example, is called P'I and stands for "stagnation." Tradition says this means that whatever course of action you are contemplating will be obstructed by evil-doers, that you are out of tune with the forces of heaven, and that it would be better to sit tight and do nothing.

If you want to get a feel for what it would be like to try to interpret the alethiometer without Lyra's special skill, you could look up the commentaries in the I Ching and try to make sense of them. Notice how they can have different meanings depending on how you choose to interpret them. Most people would say that the reason why things like the I Ching can help you solve puzzles about your own life is simply that they make you think clearly about the question you want to ask, and then you have to think hard about the answers to work out what is best for you.

You could do this on your own, making decisions for yourself, if you tried hard enough—which is something else Lyra learns as she gets older. In our world, oracles like this can't really tell the future, and they don't really communicate with forces from other worlds. They help us to communicate with our own unconscious minds. The snag is, nobody is quite sure just how the unconscious mind works.

IT'S ALL IN THE MIND

Different scientists have different ideas about how the mind works. The idea that fits right in to the story of Lyra and the golden compass comes from Carl Gustav Jung, who was born in Switzerland and lived from 1875 to 1961. The first person who really tried to understand the mind in a scientific way was an Austrian, Sigmund Freud, who lived from 1856 to 1939. He invented the idea of psychoanalysis. This tries to explain the way people behave by finding out what is going on in the unconscious part of the mind, which we are not usually aware of. The unconscious involves things like feelings, emotions, and memories that we don't think about consciously, but that are still there somehow inside our heads. Things like dreams, and slips of the tongue when we say one thing but mean to say something else, show what is going on in the unconscious. This kind of mistake is sometimes called a Freudian slip.

If Mrs. Bloggs comes to visit your family for tea, you might think that she looks like a warthog, but you are much too polite to say so. Then, while you are handing a plate of cookies around, you suddenly say to her, without meaning to, "Would you like a warthog, Mrs. Cookie?" That would be a Freudian slip—the real truth popping out without you consciously meaning to say it.

FREUD AND JUNG

Analyzing dreams, Freudian slips, and so on to try to understand the unconscious mind is part of psychoanalysis. Freud's big idea was that if someone was mentally ill, or anxious and depressed without there seeming to be any good reason, psychoanalysis could get to the root of their mental problems and help them to get better.

Jung was very interested in Freud's ideas and developed them further. He was much younger than Freud, so he learned a lot from him, and they worked together for a time. At first, they were good friends, but later on they disagreed about how to understand the unconscious and stopped working together.

One of the problems was that Freud tried to explain everything in terms of sex. For example, a lot of people are afraid of snakes. According to Freud, these fears aren't really about snakes but are something to do with the penis, which looks a bit like a snake. Jung had a different explanation. He said people are afraid of snakes because some snakes really are dangerous. But he was curious to know why even people who lived in modern cities and had never seen a snake were still frightened by the idea of snakes.

MEMORIES FROM ANCIENT DAYS

Jung came up with an idea he called the "collective unconscious." Freud said that we each have our own personal unconscious that affects the way we behave; Jung said that we all share a collective unconscious, built up from all the memories, emotions, and patterns of behavior that have grown up over the entire history of humankind. Our ancestors who lived in the forests and plains of Africa millions of years ago had every reason to be afraid of snakes. According to Jung, it is that ancestral fear that has become part of the collective unconscious, so that even city dwellers today are afraid of snakes.

But Jung didn't stop with the idea of this kind of inherited unconscious memory. He thought that the collective unconscious was part of all living people today and that it could influence the minds of people far apart from one another, especially through dreams. He thought this could explain strange coincidences and account for reports of telepathic communication, when somebody seems to know what someone else far away is doing without any communication between them.

In one famous example, Jung used to tell the story of a patient who was describing a dream involving a golden scarab beetle. Just at that moment, there was a tapping sound on the window, and when Jung opened it, a beetle flew in. He called such seemingly meaningful coincidences "synchronicities." It's like when you are thinking of phoning a friend, and then they phone you just before you get around to it. We all know the feeling. But how many times do you think about phoning somebody, and they don't call you first? It's hard to be sure whether synchronicities really do mean anything, or if they are just coincidences. But for the sake of a story like *His Dark Materials*, this doesn't matter, and we can believe in the synchronicities, and much more besides.

Is Dust conscious?

You could say that it was synchronicity that Lyra decided to trespass in the Retiring Room the very day that Lord Asriel, unknown to her, had returned to Oxford. But what put the idea into her head?

In *His Dark Materials*, the Dust is like Jung's collective unconscious. It knows what is going on everywhere, and it can make people aware of what is going on, but only indirectly, through dreams, or the I Ching, or Mary Malone's computer, or the alethiometer. Jung was fascinated by the I Ching and used it with his patients during psychoanalysis. Perhaps this helped him to communicate with the collective unconscious. Or perhaps it is another example of the power of the I Ching to make people think carefully about their problems and work out the solutions for themselves, or with the help of a psychoanalyst.

Mind you, there are people who think that Jung could have done with the help of a psychoanalyst himself. He believed that he had his own spirit companion, a kind of angel that he called Philemon. Nobody else could see Philemon, so he wasn't like a dæmon in Lyra's world, but he seemed real to Jung, who would walk up and down the garden with Philemon discussing philosophy. Psychoanalysts would say that Jung was actually talking to himself, or that in some way his conscious mind was talking to his unconscious mind. Philemon is similar to the kinds of delusions experienced by people with an illness called schizophrenia.

None of this seems very much like the kind of science we learn about in school. That's all about things we can see, and touch, and smell. Things like falling weights, or chemical experiments, or studying how plants grow from seeds. Things that we can prove are real, by measuring them. The idea that everything is made of real, hard atoms doesn't seem to have anything to do with ideas like synchronicity. But in the twentieth century, just at the same time as Jung was developing his new ideas about how the mind works, scientists were developing a new way of understanding the world of atoms and particles.

THE MAGIC OF SCIENCE

This new kind of science is called quantum physics. Quantum physics explains how the chips in a computer work, how the DNA molecules in living things work to keep those things alive, how nuclear power stations generate heat, how lasers work, and lots more besides. But quantum physics also says that the world of atoms and particles is every bit as strange as the worlds of *His Dark Materials*. This isn't surprising, because the trilogy is based on quantum physics.

Jung was very interested in the new physics, and many of the quantum physicists were interested in his work. He was particularly friendly with the physicist Wolfgang Pauli, who lived from 1900 to 1958 and won the Nobel Prize for his work in 1945. Jung and Pauli were especially interested in the way quantum physics seemed to explain synchronicity. Synchronicity is important in the third part of the trilogy, *The Amber Spyglass*, and we'll get to this later (Chapter Ten). It's in the second part of the trilogy, *The Subtle Knife*, that we understand properly that Lyra's world is just one world among many, including what seems to be our own world, and that Will and Lyra learn to travel between these worlds. Did you think this was pure fantasy? If you did, you were wrong. The whole Many Worlds idea, as we are about to see, is straight out of quantum physics.

CHAPTER FIVE

OTHER WORLDS

WORLDS BEYOND THE WORLD, AND THE QUANTUM CAT

"I think I can safely say that nobody understands quantum mechanics....Do not keep saying to yourself, if you can possibly avoid it, 'But how can it be like that?' because you will go 'down the drain' into a blind alley from which nobody has yet escaped. Nobody knows how it can be like that."

RICHARD FEYNMAN

She reached out a paw to pat something in the air in front of her, something quite invisible to Will. Then she leaped backward, back arched and fur on end, tail held out stiffly. Will knew cat behavior. He watched more alertly as the cat approached the spot again, just an empty patch of grass between the hornbeams and the bushes of a garden hedge, and patted the air once more.

Again she leaped back, but less far and with less alarm this time. After another few seconds of sniffing, touching, and whisker twitching, curiosity overcame wariness.

The cat stepped forward and vanished.

An anonymous cat is one of the most important characters in the *His Dark Materials* trilogy. First it shows Will the way to the window that opens between his Oxford and Cittàgazze. Then it draws the attention of Will and Lyra to the stone tower, the Tower of the Angels, where they find Giacomo Paradisi. There, Will becomes the bearer of the knife, after a desperate fight with Tullio in which two of Will's fingers are cut off. Finally, the cat saves them by distracting Sir Charles Latrom and Mrs. Coulter as Lyra and Will escape from Will's world.

An anonymous cat is also one of the most important characters in the story of quantum physics. This cat is a mythical beast invented by the physicist Erwin Schrödinger, an Austrian who lived from 1887 to 1961. And his cat is part of the scientific story of how other worlds really might exist alongside our own.

In search of the quantum world

Schrödinger was one of the pioneers of quantum physics, who worked out the rules that govern the behavior of things like atoms and electrons, during the 1920s. They worked these rules out partly by looking at the way different kinds of atoms (different elements) radiate light of different colors. And they also studied things like radioactivity. In radioactivity, atoms of one element spit out tiny particles and turn themselves into atoms of another element.

There is no doubt that the rules of quantum physics worked out in the 1920s are right. We know this because you can use them to predict how atoms will behave, and you can test the predictions with experiments.

That's what science is all about. If you have an idea about how the world works, you test the idea with experiments and only keep the ideas that pass the tests. That's what William Gilbert did, all those centuries ago. This is why science is different from religion. Before we had science, people thought that the way the world worked—things like planets going around the Sun—was the way it was because God wanted it to be like that. And people weren't allowed to ask why God wanted it like that or how it worked.

STRANGER THAN FICTION

But even though they pass all the tests experimenters can think of, the quantum rules are very strange. They don't match the "common sense" view of the world that we get from everyday life. Physicists have been arguing about how we can understand the quantum rules ever since they were discovered. Different physicists have different explanations, called interpretations. It's a bit like Freud and Jung arguing about the interpretation of dreams.

Schrödinger dreamed up an imaginary experiment involving his mythical cat in order to show how strange these interpretations really are. The standard way of thinking about quantum physics (especially in the twentieth century) is called the Copenhagen Interpretation, because most of it was worked out by scientists in that city. There are two crucial things about the quantum world that any good theory has to explain. The first one is called quantum probability. According to the quantum rules, nothing is certain in the quantum world. Things happen by chance, but there are rules of chance. It's like rolling dice. There are six numbers on each die, and if it is properly balanced, there is a 1 in 6 chance of each of those numbers coming up. You can't say in advance which one will come up; whatever number came up last time, there is still a 1 in 6 chance of any of the numbers coming up next time.

If you have two dice, there are different ways of

getting different numbers. You can only get 12 one way, with two sixes; but you can get 11 two ways, with 5 on the first die and 6 on the second, or 6 on the first die and 5 on the second. So if you roll two dice together, you are twice as likely to get 11 as you are to get 12. There are even more ways to get 10. Either 6+4, or 4+6, or 5+5 will do, and so on.

In with a chance

Quantum probability is more complicated still, because you are dealing with lots of atoms, but there are still proper rules of statistics that you can use to work out what is going on. And there's one very neat example, involving radioactivity.

If you have a lot of radioactive atoms of the same element, the quantum rules tell you that exactly half of them will spit out a particle and turn into another kind of atom in a certain amount of time. This process is called radioactive decay. The rules are very complicated, and we don't have room to explain them here. But the important thing is that they have all been tested by experiments and they pass the tests.

So they are definitely scientific rules, not rules of magic or religion.

The time involved in radioactive decay is called the half-life, because half the atoms decay in one half-life. And the half-life is different for each kind of radioactive element. For radioactive carbon, for example, the half-life is 5,730 years. For some radioactive elements it is much longer (millions of years), and for some it is much shorter (a split second).

It doesn't matter when you start counting, or how many radioactive atoms there are. After one half-life, half of the radioactive atoms that were there when you started will have gone. If you had a box containing 512,000 atoms of radioactive carbon, after 5,730 years there would be 256,000 left. After another half-life, half of those atoms would have decayed, so after 11,460 years there would be 128,000 radioactive carbon atoms left. After yet another 5,730 years, there would be 64,000 atoms of radioactive carbon left, and so on.

But you can never tell just when any particular atom will decay. If you sit and watch just one atom out of all the 512,000 in the box, it might decay right away, or it might still be sitting there after every other radioactive atom in the box has decayed, or it might decay at any time in between. You can only say what the chance is that it will decay in a year, or 1,000 years, or whatever. It's like throwing the die—you know there is a 1 in 6 chance of the number 6 coming up, but no matter how often you throw it you can't say whether it will be a 6 next time or not. It's completely random.

WATCH WHAT YOU'RE DOING

The other strange thing about the quantum world, according to the Copenhagen Interpretation, is that nothing is real unless you look at it. Even stranger, the nature of something like an electron changes according to how you look at it. Strictly speaking, what matters isn't looking at it but detecting it. But it amounts to the same thing. The experiments show us that an electron doesn't behave like a particle all the time. When it is moving, it behaves like a wave.

Scientists can see this in experiments where

electrons are fired, one at a time, at a screen with two tiny holes in it. The detectors on the other side of the screen show that the electrons behave as if they each spread out into a wave, like ripples on a pond, that goes through both holes at once. But where the electrons are detected, each one hits the

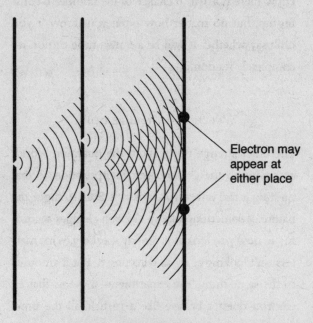

Electron may appear at either place

An electron going through two holes as a wave and then collapsing into a particle.

detector like a little bullet, as if it had turned back into a particle. The way the wave seems to turn into a particle is called the "collapse of the wave function." The Copenhagen Interpretation says that everything exists as a kind of wave, except when it is noticed. According to this interpretation, the real world is actually made real by observers like us looking at it.

Don't worry if this seems weird. It is weird. Nobody understands how the quantum world can be like this, and even the scientists don't really know what is going on. Don't just take our word for it. One of the cleverest scientists of the twentieth century, Richard Feynman, got a Nobel Prize for quantum physics, and even he said, "Nobody understands quantum theory." That's why we have to be careful to keep saying electrons behave "as if" they were a wave or a particle. We don't know what they really are.

CONFUSED ATOMS

Schrödinger realized that the collapse of the wave function affects things like radioactive atoms as well.

Imagine watching a single atom and waiting for it to decay. The statistical rules tested by experiments will tell you that there is a certain probability (like the probability of getting a 6 when you roll a die) that the atom will decay after a certain time. There might be a 1 in 10 chance that it will decay in half an hour, or a 9 in 10 chance that it will decay in a day, and so on. There will be a certain time when there is an exact 50:50 chance that the atom has decayed. If you are watching it, either it decays or it doesn't, and the moment goes past. But what if you are not watching it?

At that moment when there is a 50:50 chance of the atom decaying, according to the Copenhagen Interpretation, it is in a confused state, a wave that can't make up its mind whether to decay or not. The wave could collapse one way, so the atom decays, or it might collapse the other way, so the atom doesn't decay. But it hasn't yet done either. It isn't hard to think of an atom as being in such a mixed state, because we don't know what atoms look like anyway. So nobody worried about it until Schrödinger dreamed up his mythical experiment.

We should say that nobody has ever done this experiment, so no cats have been harmed—it is "all in the mind," what's known as a thought experiment.

COLLAPSING CATS

Schrödinger imagined a radioactive atom in this mixed state in a locked room with a live cat. A single radioactive atom couldn't hurt the cat. But if there was a machine in the room that could monitor radioactivity, even from a single atom, the machine could be attached to some gruesome device that would kill the cat if the atom decayed. Schrödinger asked, what state is the cat in when the atom is in the 50:50 state and hasn't yet decided whether it has collapsed or not?

According to the Copenhagen Interpretation, nothing is real until you look at it. If someone opens the door and looks in, they will either see a dead cat or a live cat. But if nobody looks, according to this interpretation, all the parts of the experiment—the atom, the machine, the gruesome device, and the cat—are in the mixed state, waiting to collapse when somebody opens the door. It is as if the cat is neither dead nor alive. Or as if it is alive and dead at the same time.

The really weird thing is, the same rules and equations that say you can have a cat that is dead and alive at the same time are the rules and equations that explain how computers, and lasers, and DNA work. People actually use those rules to design computers and lasers and to do genetic engineering. If the rules weren't right, none of that stuff would work. Nobody has tried to do the Schrödinger's cat "experiment," but the same rules seem to predict how it would work out.

But nobody believes cats can really be dead and alive at the same time. So what's going on?

Many Worlds

The best explanation is another quantum interpretation, called the Many-Worlds Interpretation. Instead of saying that nothing is real unless you look at it, the Many-Worlds Interpretation says that everything is real, even when you don't look at it.

How does it explain the cat puzzle? Like this. Instead of saying that the atom sits in a mixed-up state without deciding whether to decay or not, the Many-Worlds Interpretation says that it does both! It says that the whole world (the whole Universe) splits in two. In one world, the atom decays and the cat dies. In the other world, there is no decay and the cat lives. In one world, you open the door and see a dead cat; in the other world, you open the door and see a live cat. So there are also two "yous" and two of everybody and everything else. All because a single atom had the choice of whether to decay or not.

According to the Many-Worlds Interpretation, this splitting happens every time anything in the quantum world is faced with a choice. So there are millions and millions of worlds, all different from one another, which somehow exist side by side, or on top of one another. The differences might be very small (a dead cat in one world, a live cat in another). Or they might be very big.

The witches in *His Dark Materials* know all about

the Many Worlds. Kaisa, the goose dæmon of the witch Serafina Pekkala, tells Lyra that:

"You can see them sometimes in the Northern Lights. They aren't part of this universe at all; even the furthest stars are part of this universe, but the lights show us a different universe entirely. Not further away, but interpenetrating with this one. Here, on this deck, millions of other universes exist, unaware of one another...."

Making worlds

It isn't just radioactive atoms that "make" other worlds in this way. Your brain runs on electricity, for example. So there are electrons in your brain that have to obey the quantum rules. The way the electrons move around affects the way you think. So what people do is affected by the quantum rules. Have you ever been of two minds about what to do? Maybe then you know what it is like to be a radioactive atom in a mixed state! Some people think that the splitting of worlds happens whenever we make decisions, as well as when things like atoms decay. So if you decide to put this book down and go to eat a cookie, there will be another world in which you decide to stay here and finish the chapter first.

Did you eat the cookie? Perhaps you just made another world. It probably won't be very different from our world, but sometimes what people do can have a big influence on history. In

Splitting worlds.

our world, for example, Duke William of Normandy conquered England in 1066, and the English King Harold was killed at the Battle of Hastings. But if the Many-Worlds Interpretation is correct, there must be other worlds in which King Harold wasn't killed, the Norman Conquest never happened, and England became a very different place. Every possible result of every single event in history really has happened, and every world is real, according to this idea, even if we can't see it.

In our world, by the way, the Many-Worlds Interpretation of quantum physics was put forward in 1957 by Hugh Everett, an American who lived from 1930 to 1982. He gets a name check in *The Subtle Knife*, but he was a real scientist in our Universe. But although Everett made the idea of parallel universes respectable science, it had been used in science-fiction stories long before then. Unfortunately, most of the stories weren't very good. Since 1957, though, there have been a lot of good stories about parallel worlds, or alternative-history stories, where some small difference in history has changed the entire world. One of the best is *Pavane*, by Keith Roberts. If you liked the *His Dark Materials* trilogy, you'll probably like that as well.

In a way, all stories are about parallel worlds, or alternative histories. There wasn't really a detective called Sherlock Holmes, for example. At least, there wasn't one in our world. Perhaps there really is a Sherlock Holmes in one of the Many Worlds. Without going there, we can never know.

That's the problem with all this, even if the Many-Worlds Interpretation is correct. In order to get to the world next door, and to the worlds farther away, you would have to travel sideways, somehow, in a direction that is at right angles to all of the three dimensions of space. We all know about moving in three dimensions. You can go up and down, left and right, or forward and back. You can get to anywhere on Earth (or in the Universe) by moving in these three dimensions. Each direction is at right angles to the other two. But the other worlds are in a different direction from any of them. Try imagining a direction at right angles to all three of the usual dimensions, then moving in that direction! It would be much easier if you had a door, or a window, that opened from our world right into one of the other worlds.

That's where the subtle knife comes in. And, like so much of the story, the knife itself is based on real science.

Chapter Six

The Subtle Knife

Hidden dimensions, and how to cut them

✦

"When it comes to atoms, language
can be used only as in poetry.
The poet, too, is not nearly so concerned with
describing facts as with creating images."

Niels Bohr

... a swirl of cloudy colors seemed to live just under the surface of the metal: bruise purples, sea blues, earth browns, cloud grays, and the deep green under heavy-foliaged trees, the clustering shades at the mouth of a tomb as evening falls over a deserted graveyard.... If there was such a thing as shadow colored, it was the blade of the subtle knife.

But the edges were different. In fact the two edges differed from each other. One was clear bright steel, merging a little way back into those subtle shadow-colors, but steel of an incomparable sharpness. Will's eye shrank back from looking at it, so sharp did it seem. The other edge was just as keen, but silvery in color....

◆

After his fight with Tullio in the Tower of Angels, Will is taught how to use the subtle knife by Giacomo Paradisi. He learns that the knife is so sharp that it will cut through anything; one edge of the blade is infinitely thin. Even the thinnest real knife in our world would have to have an edge one atom thick, because everyday matter (baryonic matter) is made of atoms. If it were one atom thick, that would mean it could cut through the gaps between atoms, slicing anything made of ordinary baryonic matter into the tiniest pieces, as long as it never got blunt. The first edge of the subtle knife, the steel edge, is like that. This is the edge that Will uses to slice through the bear Iorek Byrnison's armor. But the second edge, the silvery edge, is the one that has seemingly magical powers. Because it is infinitely thin, it can even cut into atoms themselves. It can cut through the particles inside atoms, the subatomic particles like neutrons and protons, and release whatever is inside them.

THE STRING'S THE THING

How could there be anything inside subatomic particles? Surely that must be pure fantasy? But even this turns out to be the kind of magic that becomes science once you understand it. It is another hidden truth. The only problem is that we aren't yet clever enough to make knives that can reveal the truth about what goes on inside subatomic particles. Instead, the professors in our world, who are equivalent to the experimental theologians in Lyra's world, try to work out what is going on by using computers. They make simulations, or models, of what is going on, like a very complicated computer game. The rule of the game is that what is going on inside these simulations has to make particles that look like the ones we see in the real world. It's a bit like the way pilots are trained to fly aircraft using a simulator on the ground, which responds just like a real plane. All that would be magic to Lyra, or even to Lord Asriel, but it is science to us.

The best simulations, which make particles that look just like the ones we see in the real world, say that right inside the particles there are tiny, tiny loops of something that physicists call string. These loops are actually much more like tiny elastic bands, but somehow the name "string" has stuck.

We all know how you can stretch an elastic band and twang it to make a noise, a kind of musical note. These "strings" are stretched very tight and are twanging all the time, because they are full of energy. But they don't make musical notes. Instead, if they twang one way, they look like one kind of subatomic particle, but if they twang another way, they look like a different kind of particle. All the particles we know about can be explained in this way, as if they were different notes being played on twanging loops of string.

HOW SHORT IS A PIECE OF STRING?

It's hard to get a picture in your head of just how tiny these loops are. Remember that it would take ten million atoms to stretch across the gap between two points on the edge of a postage stamp. Even an atom is 100,000 times bigger than a particle like a proton. And it would take 100 billion billion loops of string to stretch across a single proton. There isn't much point in even trying to imagine how small these strings must be. But you would certainly need a very subtle knife to cut into them!

If you did cut into them, what would you find? Prepare to have your mind truly boggled. Remember that there are three dimensions of space that make up our Universe. People sometimes talk about time as a kind of fourth dimension, so altogether you could say that we live in a four-dimensional space-time. But even four dimensions are not enough for the people who study string, who are called string theorists.

Hidden Dimensions

All the different kinds of particles we know about can be explained as different "notes" played on the vibrating strings. But the computer simulations tell us that this only works if the strings are vibrating in at least ten dimensions, not just three, or even four. How can this be? Where are the extra six dimensions hidden?

String theorists have an answer. The best way to understand it is to think of a more ordinary example. In particular, think of an ordinary garden hose.

A hose is made out of a flat sheet of plastic, rolled around to make a tube. If you pretend that the plastic is infinitely thin, it starts out as a two-dimensional sheet. It has length and breadth, but no height. An ordinary sheet of paper is also pretty much two dimensional, if you pretend it doesn't have any thickness. To make the hose, you bend the two-dimensional sheet around the third dimension. You can do the same thing with a sheet of paper. Now you have definitely got a three-dimensional piece of hose.

Imagine the piece of hose making a loop, with its two ends joined together like armbands used for swimming, so that nothing can get out of the tube inside. What would it look like from far away? Suppose your hose was lying in the garden and a bird saw it from high above. It would just look like a single line making a circle. A line has just one dimension. It has length, but no height or breadth. From a distance, your three-dimensional hose looks like a one-dimensional line. It is as if two of the dimensions have disappeared.

String theorists say that this is what has happened to the extra six dimensions in their strings. They have been rolled up (or "compactified") so that from a distance you can't see how the strings are made. They look like loops in three dimensions of space and one of time, even though they have been curled up in ten dimensions. But the tiny loops in the extra dimensions are still there, deep within atoms and subatomic particles. Another hidden truth.

SPECTRAL ESCAPEES

This is where the Specters in Cittàgazze came from. Without knowing it, the people who made the knife, the members of the Guild of the Torre degli Angeli, used its subtle blade to cut into subatomic particles, and even into the loops of string inside them, without realizing what they were doing. One of the children Lyra and Will meet in Cittàgazze tells what happened:

"...this Guild man hundreds of years ago was taking some metal apart. Lead. He was going to make it into gold. And he cut it and cut it smaller and smaller till he came to the smallest piece he could get. There ain' nothing smaller than that. So small you couldn' see it, even. But he cut that, too, and inside the smallest little bit there was *all the Specters packed in, twisted over and folded up so tight they took up no space at all. But once he cut it, bam! They whooshed out, and they been here ever since. That's what my papa said."*

In the language of science, the knife opened up the compactified dimensions. It's like slicing lengthwise down the loop of hose and laying it out flat. If you did this, you would release any creepy-crawlies, centipedes, or beetles that had crept inside the pipe and got stuck there when the ends were joined. And when the Guild did this to the strings, the Specters who lived in the extra dimensions escaped into Cittàgazze, where they fed off the souls of adults.

But this was just an accident. The real purpose of the subtle knife was to make even finer cuts. It didn't just cut matter, or string, into tiny pieces. It could cut slices in space as well, windows into the dimensions where parallel universes existed.

STRETCHING SPACE

People usually think of empty space as nothing at all, so how could you cut windows in it? But this isn't the way scientists think of empty space. Their experiments show that space has a real existence. They think of the four dimensions of space-time as something like a stretched rubber sheet full of energy. Things like galaxies, stars, and planets are like marbles rolling around on the stretched rubber sheet, making little dents as they roll along. Space is like a kind of platform, or a stage, that makes a place where all the material particles (bright stuff and dark stuff) can go about their business.

This gives people a different way of thinking about the Expanding Universe. The clusters of galaxies aren't moving through space. They are being carried farther and farther apart because the "empty space" between them is stretching.

Think of a balloon, covered in colored dots. When you blow the balloon up, the colored dots get farther apart. But they aren't moving through the rubber skin of the balloon. The rubber is stretching, so the dots get farther apart. That's like the way clusters of galaxies are carried farther apart in the Expanding Universe.

Or imagine a goldfish bowl that is steadily getting bigger, with more water appearing by magic to keep it full all the time. An inflatable fish tank, with the amount of water inside increasing by magic so that it stays full even though it is getting bigger. The fish in the bowl stay the same size and swim about quite happily in the water. But their "universe" is expanding.

WORLDS WITHIN WORLDS

One way of thinking about the Many Worlds described in Chapter Five is to imagine millions and millions of balloons, one inside the other like those nested Russian dolls, each one made of its own stretchy space. When Will cuts a window in space in one world, it opens into one of the other worlds. There is another Earth "underneath" our Earth, and another one under that, and so on forever. And there is another Earth "on top of" our Earth, and another one on top of that, and so on forever. They stay next door to each other even though the "balloons" are expanding because they are all expanding at the same rate. So once Will cuts a window, it stays in the same place in both worlds. But each balloon is a different space-time.

But there's one more thing about space-time. It's just like the way things that seem solid in the everyday world, like the skin of a balloon, are actually made of little pieces called atoms, and just like the way something that looks like a solid line from a distance, like a hose, can be opened up when you look closely. Quantum physics tells us that space-time isn't really smooth and continuous, like rubber. It's more like a fabric that has been woven, like cotton. It has been woven out of another kind of quantum string. Everybody knows you can unpick the threads of woven fabric using the point of a very sharp knife. Because he is the knife bearer, Will can unpick the fabric of space-time using the subtle knife.

"Think about the knife tip. That is where you are. Now feel with it, very gently. You're looking for a gap so small you could *never see it with your eyes, but the knife tip will find it, if you put your mind there. Feel along the air till you sense the smallest little gap in the world. . . ."*

It was like delicately searching out the gap between one stitch and the next with the point of a scalpel. He touched, withdrew, touched again to make sure, and then did as the old man had said, and cut sideways with the silver edge.

That's how Will is able to cut windows in space-time, windows that open into other worlds, the Many Worlds of quantum reality, nested inside each other like Russian dolls.

But even this isn't the whole story. Remember that scientists think about the four dimensions of space-time, not just the three dimensions of space, as making up this kind of stretchy fabric. If you could cut a hole in space, you could also cut a hole in time—a window into the past or the future! We'll leave that idea for Philip Pullman to use in another book. Now that we've explained how it might be possible to travel to other earths, though, we ought to try to understand why some worlds (like Lyra's and Will's) are very similar to one another, but some, like our world and the world where Mary Malone meets the wheeled creatures, are so different from one another. It's all a matter of balance.

CHAPTER SEVEN

THE WORLDS OF IF

THE POWER OF CHOICE, AND
A BALANCING ACT

✦

"TIME IS THAT GREAT GIFT OF NATURE WHICH
KEEPS EVERYTHING FROM HAPPENING AT ONCE."
C. J. OVERBECK

"...the men came to look and broke into the house again. It was nighttime, or early morning. And I was hiding at the top of the stairs and Moxie—my cat, Moxie—she came out of the bedroom. And I didn't see her, nor did the man, and when I knocked into him she tripped him up, and he fell right to the bottom of the stairs...."

"And I ran away. That's all that happened. So I didn't mean to kill him, but I don't care if I did. I ran away and went to Oxford and then I found that window. And that only happened because I saw the other cat and stopped to watch her, and she found the window first. If I hadn't seen her... or if Moxie hadn't come out of the bedroom then...."

❖

Like Will, everybody has "what if" moments. What would have happened if I hadn't gone to the movies last week but had done my homework instead? Or "if only"—if only I'd bought the first hardcover edition of the first Harry Potter book, I could have sold it now and been rich. There are lots of stories about worlds where things turned out differently from our world because "what if" moments turned out a different way. In Chapter Five, we saw how the Many-Worlds Interpretation of quantum physics says that all these possible worlds are real, parallel universes that somehow exist "next door" to our own Universe. You might think that it would take a big change, like King Harold winning the Battle of Hastings in 1066, to make a new world that was very different from our own. But you'd be wrong. Sometimes, very small changes can have very big effects.

İn THE BALAnCE

It all depends how delicately balanced things are. Suppose you decided to stay in bed for an extra ten minutes one morning. You wouldn't think that would change the world very much, and most days you'd be right. But suppose that on this particular day, just during those few minutes, a meteorite hit the house and killed you. That would be a pretty big change as far as you were concerned. And suppose that in the world where you got up on time, you went on to become a great scientist and find a cure for some terrible disease. In that case, the two worlds—one where you stayed in bed and one where you didn't—would end up very different from each other.

This is an unlikely scenario. But remember that according to the Many-Worlds Interpretation, every possible thing happens in one of the infinite number of parallel worlds. So it is very unlikely that you will be struck by a meteorite in any one world, but it is absolutely certain that some version of "you" will be struck by a meteorite in one of the Many Worlds!

If a very small change in something has a very big effect on the way the world turns out, the world is said to be "sensitive to initial conditions." Things have to be balanced in just the right way for this to happen.

After the subtle knife is broken, and before Iorek mends it, Lyra asks the alethiometer whether it should be mended or not. The answer she gets tells her how delicately the fate of all the worlds depends on what she chooses to do:

"I never known it so confused....there was lots of things it said. I think I got it clear. I think so. It said about balance first. It said the knife could be harmful or it could do good, but it was so slight, such a delicate kind of balance, that the faintest thought or wish could tip it one way or the other....and it meant you, Will, it meant what you wished or thought, only it didn't say what would be a good thought or a bad one."

The kind of balancing involved is like the fate of a raindrop that falls on a high mountain ridge in the Rocky Mountains. If it falls on one side of the ridge, it will trickle away westward into a stream that becomes a river flowing into the Pacific Ocean. If it falls just a fraction of an inch away on the other side of the ridge, it will end up in the Atlantic Ocean, thousands of miles away. The fate of the drop is "sensitive to initial conditions," all right, but in this case the world doesn't really care.

WEATHER, OR NOT

One feature of the World that sometimes cares a lot about initial conditions is the weather.

Meteorologists know this because they can simulate the weather on their computers. They put in all the numbers corresponding to the real temperature, pressure, and so on for today, then run the computer model to see what the weather will be like tomorrow. Just out of curiosity, some meteorologists tried changing some of the numbers a tiny bit and running the models again. They found that sometimes it doesn't make much difference to the forecast. But sometimes it makes a huge difference. On those days, when it makes a huge difference, the weather is sensitive to initial conditions.

In addition to all these tiny variations, the meteorologists can never be certain that every single number they put into their models has been measured exactly right. If you ever have to key in a long stream of numbers, even a password that you think you know by heart, you soon realize how easy it is to make a slight mistake. Even one mistyped figure can make a huge difference to your final calculation. So sometimes the weather forecast is very accurate, and sometimes it is useless. It just depends how the weather is balanced that day.

One small thing that could have an influence on the weather is the way a butterfly flaps its wings. If it sits still for a minute before flapping away from a flower, there will be a tiny difference from if it sits still for two minutes before flapping away. A bit whimsically, meteorologists imagine that the way a butterfly flaps its wings in Brazil might make it rain over London several days later. But if it doesn't flap, the weather in London will be fine. Because of this, the whole business about being sensitive to initial conditions is often called the Butterfly Effect.

WORLDS WITHIN WORLDS

But surely this kind of effect wouldn't matter if we had perfect computers and we measured all the temperatures and so on exactly, would it? Then the forecasts would be spot-on every time, no matter how sensitive the weather was to initial conditions.

The snag is, you can't measure all the numbers perfectly. In fact, sometimes you can't even measure one number perfectly!

Think of a number like pi (π). Some numbers involving fractions are said to be rational, because they can be written as a ratio of two ordinary whole numbers. So a half is $1/2$, which you can also write as 0.5; three-quarters is $3/4$, or 0.75; and so on. You could even write $21/7$ instead of 3, if you felt like it. But a number like π is said to be irrational, because there is no ratio of whole numbers (integers) that will give you the exact value of π. We sometimes use $22/7$ to represent π if we are doing rough calculations, but this is only an approximation.

Why should we care about π? Pi is important because it comes up in lots of things in nature. It is a measure of the ratio of the circumference of a circle (any circle) to its diameter. So anywhere there are circles, there is π. And it comes up in other places, including the equations that describe electromagnetism and the equations of quantum physics. You couldn't design TV systems, or lasers, without knowing about π.

If you try to write π out as a decimal, it begins 3.1415926535, and it goes on forever. Literally forever, with an infinite number of numbers after the decimal point. If π comes up in a calculation, you have to chop it off somewhere. So you might decide to use 3.1415926, and leave it at that. But if the calculation involves something like the weather, and the weather is in a very sensitively balanced state, you would get a completely different forecast if you went one place further and used 3.14159265, or if you went one place back and used 3.141592. It isn't even necessarily true that you get a more accurate answer by using more places of decimals.

There are lots of irrational numbers like π (in fact, there is an infinite number of them), and they turn up all the time in calculations. And there are a lot of things like the weather that are very sensitive to initial conditions, at least some of the time. But if you wanted to store just one of these irrational numbers exactly in your computer, the computer would have to have an infinitely big memory. So it is absolutely impossible to make perfect forecasts of anything at all. We can only make approximate forecasts. And if things are very sensitive to initial conditions, the forecasts will be useless.

TILTING THE SCALES

That's why Lyra's quest is so important, even though she seems like an insignificant child caught up between the two powerful forces of the Authority on one side and Lord Asriel on the other. What she does has a huge effect on the worlds, like the butterfly flapping its wings in Brazil and changing the weather over London. Everything is balanced very delicately, and what Lyra and Will do determines the outcome of the whole battle.

If you had an old-fashioned balance scale, it could be perfectly balanced with a huge weight in one scale pan and the same huge weight on the other side. Just adding a single feather would make the balance tilt one way. Lyra and Will are like that single feather, tilting the balance in favor of Lord Asriel's forces.

This is another example of a hidden truth buried in Philip Pullman's story. He is telling us that the decisions we make, even small decisions, affect the future. One way of putting this is to say that we have free will. People used to think that what human beings did was laid down by the gods and that we were like puppets doing what they wanted. Stories from ancient Greece, like the story of Odysseus, are built on this idea that what we do is determined by Fate. Everything was said to be pre-ordained by Fate, so that even if you thought you had a choice (even about something as trivial as lying in bed for an extra few minutes), it had all been decided for you in advance by the gods.

MAKING YOUR MIND UP

When science began, people like Isaac Newton also thought that everything was pre-ordained. They thought the rules of science worked like a kind of clockwork. They thought the Universe had been "wound up" in the beginning and that everything that has happened since would have been as predictable as the ticking of a clock, if you had been around in the beginning and you were clever enough to work it all out.

Modern science tells us that this is not so. In a sense, because of sensitivity to initial conditions, the Universe itself doesn't "know" what is going to happen next. Human decisions really are made with free will, and they really do affect the whole World. Sometimes the effects are small; sometimes they are big. But they are real. Every single person matters. We are free to make our own decisions about what we do with our lives.

Systems that are extremely sensitive to initial conditions are said to be chaotic. This isn't what most people mean by chaos. To most people, chaos just means a mess. But in a scientific context, chaos is when something is very sensitive to initial conditions and is unpredictable. It is when a tiny change in something today can have a big effect on what happens tomorrow. And that is why some of the worlds that Will and Lyra visit are so very different from their own worlds.

WHEN WORLDS DIVERGE

The differences between Lyra's and Will's own worlds are really quite small. Mostly, Lyra's world doesn't have as much technology as Will's world—no cars, or airplanes, or TV. But they both have Oxfords, with colleges and professors and students (even if there is no Jordan College in Will's world). They even have the same bench in the same park in each Oxford.

Something different must have happened long ago to make the two worlds different, but it didn't have a big effect. The worlds weren't very sensitive to that particular change. You can imagine for yourself what kind of change would have made the kind of differences described in the story. Perhaps the two worlds were the same up until the time of Queen Elizabeth I, and then, in what became Lyra's world, the Spanish Armada succeeded in invading England.

But the world of the *mulefa* is very different from either Lyra's world or Will's world. The change that made that world must have happened at a particularly sensitive time, and very long ago indeed—probably long before the time of the dinosaurs.

İnfinite possibilities

Could anything at all happen in one of the Many Worlds? Not necessarily. Just because we can imagine something doesn't mean it is possible. If the Many-Worlds Interpretation is right, anything possible can happen in one of the Many Worlds. In fact, if anything happens once, and there is an infinite number of worlds, then there must be an infinite number of worlds where it happens! Infinity plus infinity is still infinity.

There's a neat example to show just how weird infinity is. Imagine a hotel that has an infinite number of rooms, and all the rooms are full. If someone arrives at the hotel and wants a room, all the receptionist has to do is move the person in Room One into Room Two, the person in Room Two into Room Three, and so on. Then the new guest can stay in Room One.

Or suppose that an infinite number of new guests arrive. All the receptionist has to do is move the guest in Room One into Room Two, the guest in Room Three into Room Six, the guest in Room Five into Room Ten, and so on. The guest who was in Room Two has to go in Room Four, so the guest who was in Room Four has to go in Room Eight, and so on, and so on. After all the moves, an infinite number of odd-numbered rooms are left empty! And you can do the whole business as often as you like—even an infinite number of times.

In an infinite hotel, you can always fit an infinite number of new guests in, even if the hotel is full. And you can do this an infinite number of times! In the same way, if there are infinite worlds, there is room for an infinite number of identical worlds, as well as an infinite number of different worlds.

But this is getting away from the story. What matters is that, according to the Many-Worlds

Interpretation, all the worlds have to be possible ones. As far as we know, it would be impossible to make a knife that literally has an infinitely sharp edge. So there couldn't really be a world containing a subtle knife. That's okay; after all, the story is supposed to be fiction!

But what about the creatures with wheels—the *mulefa*? Could there really be a world like that? Just maybe. Their way of life is an example of what's known as symbiosis, and there are plenty of living things in our World that depend on symbiosis every bit as much as the *mulefa* do.

Chapter Eight

Living Together

The nature of wheels, hummingbirds, and the living planet

✦

"The life of the individual has meaning
only insofar as it aids in making the life of
every living thing nobler and more beautiful.
Life is sacred, that is to say, it is
the supreme value, to which all other
values are subordinate."
Albert Einstein

...she began to wonder which had come first: wheel or claw? Rider or tree?

Although of course there was a third element as well, and that was geology. Creatures could only use wheels on a world that provided them with natural highways. There must be some feature of the mineral content of these stone roads that made them run in ribbon-like lines over the vast savanna, and be so resistant to weathering or cracking. Little by little, Mary came to see the way everything was linked together, and all of it, seemingly, managed by the mulefa.

✦

The mulefa are the intelligent inhabitants of the world that Mary Malone is led to by her reading of the I Ching. Like other animals in that world, they have four legs. But instead of having two in the front and two in the back, like cats and dogs or other animals in our world, their limbs are arranged in a diamond pattern. They have one at the front, one at the back, and one on either side.

So the wild animals of this world, the equivalent of our deer, "moved with a curious rocking motion."

A STRANGE PARTNERSHIP

But the *mulefa* have found a better way to get around. As well as their legs, they each have a powerful, flexible trunk, like an elephant, that they can use the way we use our hands. So they don't need hands, and their limbs are just for locomotion. They have evolved so that they can use as wheels the large circular seedpods from the great trees that grow on their world.

On each of their front and back legs, the *mulefa* have a specially adapted claw that is just the right size and shape to hook into the hole in the middle of a seedpod, like an axle connecting to a wheel, where oil from the seedpods lubricates the "bearing." And the two outer legs are used to push the creatures along as they whiz across the natural "roads," made of solidified volcanic lava, that weave across the plains of the planet—a bit like skiers using two long ski poles to push themselves across the snow.

The mulefa need the seedpods. But it turns out that the trees also need the mulefa, to enable them to reproduce and survive. The pods are so tough and hard that they only break open to release the seeds after a lot of hard pounding on the lava roads. The hard pounding happens when they are carrying their "riders" from place to place. When the seedpods crack open, the mulefa take the seeds and plant them, nurturing them so that they can grow into big, strong trees. This kind of relationship, where two kinds of living things each depend on the other for survival, is called symbiosis.

But how could this relationship get started? There must have been, long ago, ancestors of the trees that didn't need mulefa, and ancestors of the mulefa that didn't need trees. They must have evolved to become more and more dependent on each other.

THE nATURE OF nATURAL SELECTiOn

It's easy to see how this could have happened. Long ago, when the ancestors of the mulefa first discovered the trick of using circular seedpods as wheels, the individuals with the strongest claws would have been able to balance better and use the wheels more efficiently. So they would be able to get around more as well as find food, somewhere good to live, and a mate. With all those benefits, they would have lots of children who would inherit their strong claws, and some of those children might have claws that were a tiny bit stronger still.

But in each generation, individuals with weak claws who couldn't "ride" so well wouldn't have such a good life and wouldn't be able to raise as many children. They would leave fewer descendants. Over many generations, this would mean that the claws got bigger and better suited to their task. This process is called natural selection; it's how evolution works.

By the time Mary came along, in each adult individual:

The claw was formidably strong: a spur of horn or bone at right angles to the leg, and slightly curved so that the highest part, in the middle, bore the weight as it rested on the inside of the hole.

But while all this was going on and the

mulefa were evolving over millions of years, the seedpods were evolving as well. Naturally, in each generation the *mulefa* ancestors would choose the hardest, roundest pods for their wheels, and the ones with the best oil. So they would plant the seeds from these pods and ignore the others.

Over many generations, the seedpods would get rounder and harder, and more oily, until they were so hard that the only way the seeds could be released was by the pods being ridden long distances over the lava ribbons. The result was symbiosis. The two symbionts could no longer manage without each other. If the *mulefa* died out, so would the seedpod trees; if the trees died out, so would the *mulefa*.

It might seem far-fetched. But the same sort of thing has happened lots of times in our world. One beautiful example comes from hummingbirds.

Buzzing Birds

Hummingbirds are the smallest birds on Earth. Some are really tiny. Most of them live in South

America, but some species live in North America. Even the largest ones are only about eight inches long, and the smallest species, called the bee hummingbird, is just over two inches long, and half of that is taken up by its beak and tail. But even this is bigger than the actual bee-sized hummingbird that Mary Malone comes across in the world of the *mulefa*. Because they are so very small and light, hummingbirds can hover by beating their wings very fast. This makes the humming noise that gives them their name. They can hover in front of flowers and dip their beaks into the flowers to sip nectar for food.

Compared with the length of its body, a hummingbird's bill is usually very long and slender. In the sword-billed hummingbird, the bill makes up more than half of the length of the entire bird, which is about eight and a quarter inches. Why should natural selection have encouraged such long beaks to evolve? Because a bird with a longer beak can probe farther into flowers to get at the nectar. A bird with a short beak can't get as much food. Over many generations, the beaks of these birds have gotten longer than the beaks of their ancestors.

THE BIRDS AND THE FLOWERS

But what do the plants get out of all this? Just like bees, hummingbirds carry pollen from one flower to another. While the bird is hovering by a flower, poking its beak and tiny head deep into the flower to get food, it is getting dusted with pollen (usually under the beak, on its "chin"). When it flies on to feed at another plant, some of the pollen gets rubbed off, and the flower is fertilized.

It's best for the plants if the birds get covered in lots of pollen. If a plant has a very long, trumpet-shaped flower, the bird will have to push its head and bill right inside to get nectar, so it will get covered with lots of pollen. This means that this kind of plant will get fertilized easily; but plants that make it too easy to get at the food won't get pollinated. So over many generations, the flowers get longer and more trumpet-shaped, and the food gets harder to reach.

All the time, birds with longer beaks than average do best and have more descendants, and plants with longer flowers do best and have more descendants.

In some cases, this has gone so far that the beak of the bird is perfectly shaped to feed off one kind of flower but doesn't fit any other flowers; and the plant with that kind of flower has to be fertilized by that kind of bird, because no other bird has a beak that can reach its nectar. One can't live without the other. This is true of the flowering plant and the hummingbird: they have become symbionts. That has really happened in our world, even without either of the symbionts being aware of it, like the mulefa, and encouraging evolution along.

THE ROCKY ROAD TO LIFE

That's all very well for living things, where evolution can take advantage of the tiny differences between individuals that exist in each generation. But surely it's a bit far-fetched for Philip Pullman to imagine a world where convenient natural roads are laid down by flowing ribbons of lava? How could the rocks play a part in evolution?

The only cop-out might seem to be that if there really are infinitely possible worlds, then, as we have said, anything that is possible must happen somewhere. But perhaps we don't need that cop-out. Maybe the notion isn't so far-fetched, and maybe the Earth itself has a part to play in evolution on our own planet.

One of the most important chemicals for life is carbon dioxide. Plants take carbon dioxide out of the air and use sunlight and water to turn it into their tissues, leaves, seeds, and fruit. Animals feed off plants, or off other animals that feed off plants. Without carbon dioxide, we wouldn't be here. But how does carbon dioxide get into the air? And why didn't it all run out long ago?

THE CARBON DIOXIDE PUMP

Carbon dioxide is always leaking out of volcanoes. If there wasn't some way to recycle it, there would actually be more and more in the air all the time. But carbon dioxide is also leaking away all the time, because when it is dissolved in rainwater it reacts with rocks to make calcium carbonate. This gradually wears away the rocks in a process called rock weathering. The calcium carbonate washes down to the sea and gets buried in sediment at the bottom of the ocean.

Eventually, this sediment is turned into new carbonate rocks. After millions of years, these rocks get melted inside new volcanoes, and the carbon dioxide gets back into the air.

People used to think that this was just chemistry and had nothing to do with life. But about 30 years ago the English scientist Jim Lovelock discovered that rock weathering happens much faster right next to plants, because they pump carbon dioxide from the air into the soil. The amount of carbon dioxide in the air stays the same because of a process similar to trying to fill a leaky bucket up with water. The water runs into the bucket from a tap and runs out of the bottom through the hole, so the amount of water in the bucket stays the same.

So life itself is part of the carbon dioxide pump. If there were no life on Earth, the amount of carbon dioxide in the air would be much greater, because the rock weathering would be much slower. It would be like making the hole in the bucket smaller, so less water was running out than was coming in from the tap.

One effect of extra carbon dioxide would be to trap heat near the surface of the Earth. This is called the greenhouse effect. Without plants to speed up rock weathering, the planet would turn into a hot desert.

THE LIVING PLANET

There are lots of other ways in which living things on Earth influence the planet itself, and the planet in turn influences living things. The process of one thing influencing something else, which then influences the first thing, is called feedback. We all know one kind of feedback, which happens when a thermostat switch operates the central heating. When the room gets hot, the switch automatically turns the heat off. Then, when the room cools down, it turns the heat back on. So the temperature in the room always stays about the same. Scientists like Jim Lovelock have found very many feedbacks between living things and the rocks and gases that make up Planet Earth.

There are so many of these feedbacks that it seems as if everything on Earth is linked in a complicated web. Not just the living things, but rocks, and air, and clouds, and so on. Everything works together to keep the living planet going.

This is a bit like the way all the parts of your body work together to keep it going. The heart, the lungs, your liver, and so on are all working together to make a living person. But none of them can live on its own.

Perhaps the planet is like this. The whole planet is alive, but if you took one bit of life on its own (a tree, perhaps) and put it on another planet, it could not survive (just as Will could not survive for long in Lyra's world, and she could not stay in his). Lovelock calls the whole living planet Gaia, because Gaia was the Greek goddess of the Earth. His idea is that you can't have a planet that is only partly alive, just as you can't have a person who is partly alive. You can either have a dead planet, or a planet like the Earth that is full of life involved in feedbacks with the environment. What every living thing on Earth does is important to the planet as a whole—and so are lots of the things that we don't usually think of as being alive.

THE SOUL OF GAIA

In *His Dark Materials*, Dust is like the soul of Gaia. It is everywhere, and it forms a link between living things and the things we think of as being nonliving. Dust encourages links and feedbacks to develop between living things. Dust has encouraged the *mulefa* to develop their relationship with the seedpods and the giant trees. In a way, it has sped up evolution in all the worlds visited by Lyra and Will.

The *mulefa* have some understanding of this, because they can see Dust, which they call *sraf*.

Dust is leaking away, out of all the worlds, and without it the worlds will die. The only way to save the worlds is through the love Will and Lyra have for each other. But because people can't see Dust, the problem only becomes clear when Mary Malone, helped by the *mulefa*, makes a kind of telescope with which she can see what is going on—the amber spyglass.

Chapter Nine

The Amber Spyglass

How to see invisible light, and the way scientists work

✦

"The important thing in science is not so much to obtain new facts as to discover new ways of thinking about them."
Lawrence Bragg

. . .when she looked through, everything was changed. . . . Everywhere she looked she could see gold, just as Atal had described it: sparkles of light, floating and drifting and sometimes moving in a current of purpose. Among it all was the world she could see with the naked eye, the grass, the river, the trees; but wherever she saw a conscious being, one of the mulefa, the light was thicker and more full of movement. It didn't obscure their shapes in any way; if anything it made them clearer.

I didn't know it was beautiful, Mary said to Atal.

✦

The amber spyglass that Mary Malone uses to see Dust is made of two sheets of transparent lacquer, coated with oil from the seedpods, and held a little way apart in a tube, like a telescope. It sounds like pure magic—a telescope you can use to see things that are invisible to your naked eye. But like so much of the trilogy, this idea comes straight from the real science of our world. This time, it isn't even anything as way-out as dark matter. The same science that is behind the amber spyglass explains how an ordinary pair of Polaroid sunglasses works. But although the sunglasses may be ordinary, the science behind them is amazing.

SEEⅈⅡG DOUBLE

The *mulefa* make the lacquer from the sap of a kind of tree that they cultivate specially for that purpose. They use it as a varnish. By painting many coats of this lacquer onto a piece of wood or shell and letting it set, they can build up a thickness of transparent, amber-colored material. By copying this technique and then cutting away the wood at the back, Mary is left with a clear piece of lacquer, like a pane of amber-colored glass.

Why should she bother to do this? The reason she goes to all this trouble is that she has been intrigued by a curious property of the amber lacquer. When she looks through it, everything she sees is split in two, into a double image, with the right-hand one quite close to the left-hand one and about fifteen degrees upward from it. As a physicist, Mary already knows that there is something in our world that does almost exactly the same thing: a clear crystal known as Iceland spar, or calcite.

Iceland spar really does exist in our world, and people have known about it for hundreds of years, although nobody could explain what was going on until the nineteenth century. Before then, for all anybody knew, it was magic.

THE LIGHT FANTASTIC

What seems to be happening is that when light arrives at the surface of a crystal of Iceland spar, some of it goes straight on, and some of it gets bent a tiny bit to one side. This bending is called refraction. The rainbow colors of a spectrum are made when different colors of light (different wavelengths) get bent by slightly different amounts by triangular prisms made from ordinary glass or by raindrops. But the bending that goes on in Iceland spar is different. It doesn't have anything to do with color or wavelength. It just takes half the light, whatever its color, and shifts it to one side.

That's curious enough. But what would you expect to see if you sent the doubled beam of light through another crystal of Iceland spar? Obviously, you might think, each of the two beams would be split in two, and you'd get four images.

But you'd be wrong! Instead of splitting up the light even more, the second crystal joins the two

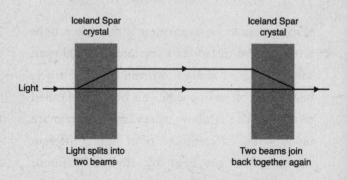

Iceland spar.

beams of light back together, so that you get a single image, just as if you were looking through a sheet (or two sheets) of ordinary flat window glass.

THE DOUBLENESS DISAPPEARS

That's exactly what Mary discovers when she puts two pieces of the amber lacquer together:

The amber color was denser, and like a photographic filter it emphasized some colors and held back others, giving a slightly different cast to the landscape. The curious thing was that the doubleness had disappeared, and everything was single again; but there was no sign of Shadows.

Mary isn't at all surprised at the way the doubleness disappears, because she knows about Iceland spar. She expects the doubleness to disappear. And this is very encouraging for her, because she knows that in our world the doubleness is caused by something called polarization, and she has the idea that polarization might help her to see Shadows—what the *mulefa* call *sraf*.

Polarization has to do with the way light moves, like a wave. Waves of light are like ripples on a pond, going up and down, or like waves on the sea. With light, though, the thing that is doing the waving is the electromagnetic field, discovered by William Gilbert all those centuries ago.

If you have a rope, and you tie one end tight to a tree and pull the other end to keep the rope tight, you can send little ripples along the rope by jiggling the end in your hand. Light is like that. It is ripples of electromagnetism. The light waves are actually made by electrons jiggling around inside atoms, which is why each kind of atom makes its own color (wavelength) of light. But instead of just jiggling up and down, light waves can wiggle from side to side at any angle.

LIGHT WITH ATTITUDE

You can make your rope wiggle any way you want it to. Up and down, or horizontally, or at any angle in between. The neat thing about ordinary light is that it does all these different wiggles at once. It is vibrating vertically, and from side to side, and at all the angles in between, all at the same time. But when it comes to a crystal of Iceland spar, it can't do this anymore.

If there was a picket fence, with vertical posts, between you and the tree your rope was fastened to, and the rope had to go through one of the gaps in the fence, you wouldn't be able to make it ripple right down to the tree in a sideways direction anymore. If you tried to make it ripple sideways, the ripples would only go as far as the fence, then they would be blocked off. You could only get the ripples to go all the way to the tree if you made them vertical, so that they could slip through the slot in the fence.

The atoms and molecules in a crystal line up in a very orderly pattern. The exact pattern depends on the kind of crystal. But in some cases they line up so that only light that is vibrating in a certain direction can get through them. If ordinary light shines on the crystal, the light coming out on the other side is all vibrating in the same way. This kind of light that is all jiggling just in one sideways direction is called polarized light; it is light with a certain attitude, all pointing vertically, or all horizontally, or all at the same angle in between. The wiggles on your rope going through the picket fence are like vertically polarized light.

CROSSED LIGHT

Now imagine that your rope is going through the arrow slit in a castle wall and is tied tightly on the other side. Arrow slits are made like a cross, with an up–down slot and a left–right slot, for archers to fire out of. You could make the ripples on your rope go through the vertical arrow slit by rippling them up and down or through the horizontal slit

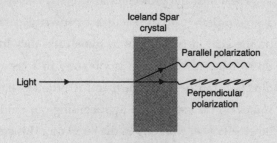

Polarization in Iceland spar.

by rippling them left and right. This is equivalent to two kinds of polarized light—vertical and horizontal polarization.

Something like this happens in Iceland spar. The pattern made by the atoms in the crystal leaves two slots for light to get through. Vertically polarized light goes one way, horizontally polarized light goes the other way, and all the other kinds of ripples are blocked off. In a second crystal, the two kinds of polarized light are joined back together again.

Ordinary Polaroid sunglasses are made of a polarizing material, although nothing quite as exciting as Iceland spar—it would be a bit confusing if they made a double image of everything you looked at! Polaroid itself is actually a thin film of nitrocellulose packed with tiny crystals all lined up in the same way, so that only one polarization of light can get through. There are other ways to make polarizing filters, as they are known, but the details don't matter here.

It just happens that when sunlight reflects off the sea or a similar shiny surface, the reflected light is naturally horizontally polarized. So polarizing sunglasses are made with vertical "slits," because no horizontally polarized light can get through. They cut out all of the reflected glare, and some of the ordinary light as well.

If you have a discarded pair of Polaroid sunglasses that nobody needs anymore, you can see how this works for yourself. If you take the lenses out and put one in front of the other but keep them oriented the way they were in the frames, the two lenses together don't make the view much darker than one lens on its own. Only vertically polarized light gets through the first lens, but since it is vertically polarized, it will all get through the second lens as well. You can do the same thing using two unbroken pairs of Polaroid sunglasses, one held in front of the other.

But if you rotate one of the lenses by 90 degrees, the polarizing filters are crossed, with one vertical and one horizontal. Now the view through the two lenses together is completely black. Only vertically polarized light gets through the first filter, but since the second filter is now horizontally polarized, none of this light at all can get through it.

Working in the dark

Mary is surprised when she learns that the mulefa can see sraf—what she calls Shadow particles—dancing in the air and that it looks to them like the sparkles cast off by ripples in the water at sunset. It is this that gives her the idea of using the lacquer lens to try to see sraf. She knows that light reflected off water is polarized, and she guesses that the lacquer affects polarized light the same way that Iceland spar does. Perhaps, she thinks, sraf looks like sparkling water because the light reflected from it is polarized.

But she is wrong. Something extra is needed before she can use the amber spyglass to see sraf.

She learns that the oil from the seed tree is somehow absorbed by the mulefa through their feet when they use the seedpods as wheels, and that this helps them to see more clearly. In particular, it helps them to see *sraf*. But she doesn't realize how this can help her, and she goes on tinkering with the amber lenses she has made, without really knowing what she is doing:

She moved the two pieces apart, watching how the appearance of things changed as she did so. When they were about a hand span apart, a curious thing happened: the amber coloring disappeared, and everything seemed its normal color, but brighter and more vivid.

This is exactly the way scientists really do work when they are fiddling around, trying to investigate something new. They try this and that, just to see what happens, and they are curious and observant about everything.

The *mulefa* are not so curious. Mary's friend Atal only wants to know if she can see *sraf* yet. When she says no but she can see other things, and tries to show Atal, Atal is only politely interested—not with *the sense of discovery that was animating Mary*—and soon gets bored. The *mulefa* just don't have the kind of scientific curiosity that makes people like Mary puzzle about everything, even when they are groping in the dark.

Seeing invisible light

Mary eventually solves her problem through a lucky accident. The name for this kind of lucky accident is serendipity. Lots of important scientific discoveries have been made by serendipity—for example, the important antibiotic penicillin was found this way—and once again Philip Pullman's story is telling us something true about the way science works.

On this occasion, Mary gets some seed oil from one of Atal's wheels on her fingers and accidentally smears some onto the lacquer. When she looks through the two lenses, a hand span apart, again:

... something had happened.

As she looked through, she saw a swarm of golden sparkles surrounding the form of Atal. They were only visible through one small part of the lacquer, and then Mary realized why: at that point she had touched the surface of it with her oily fingers.

Once she has made the discovery, it is straightforward for the mulefa to fit the two amber lenses into a short length of bamboo, keeping them a hand span apart, and for Mary to smear oil all over the lenses so that she can see sraf at any time. The amber spyglass is complete. With its help, Mary learns about the nature of Dust, and the crisis facing all the worlds, and how only Lyra and Will can save them.

We can't tell you how to make an amber spyglass that will show you Dust. But we can tell you how to make something nearly as spectacular: a spyglass that will let you see invisible light. If you take two Polaroid lenses and line them up the way we have described, like the lenses in Mary's amber spyglass, what you see through them is just our everyday world, a bit darker than it would be without the lenses in the way. But if you scrunch up a piece of cellophane (something like a clear wrapper from a piece of hard candy will do) and put it between the two lenses, you see all kinds of colors, with patterns that change as you twist the lenses.

This is pure scientific magic. It happens because the different colors of polarized light are affected differently by the cellophane. It isn't as useful as the amber spyglass, but it does really exist in our world.

Once Mary has the amber spyglass, almost all the pieces of the story are in place, and it begins to move toward its conclusion. But there is one last piece of scientific magic that plays a key role as the story develops—the "lodestone resonator," with which the Gallivespian spies instantly communicate with Lord Roke, the spymaster for Lord Asriel, even when they are in a different world from him. Surely that can't be based on real science? Oh, yes it can!

Chapter Ten

Entanglement

Love is all you need

✦

"Our death is not an end if we can live on
in our children and the younger generation.
For they are us; our bodies are only
wilted leaves on the tree of life."
Albert Einstein

"Your scientists, what do you call them, experimental theologians, would know of something called quantum entanglement. It means that two particles can exist that only have properties in common, so that whatever happens to one happens to the other at the same moment, no matter how far apart they are. Well, in our world there is a way of taking a common lodestone and entangling all its particles, and then splitting it in two so that both parts resonate together. The counterpart to this is with Lord Roke, our commander. When I play on this one with my bow, the other one reproduces the sounds exactly, and so we communicate."

It's a pity that Philip Pullman chose lodestone as the working material for the Gallivespians' resonator, because lodestone is a natural magnet, and in our world a lodestone resonator would be something that made electromagnetic waves— radio waves, like light ripples, only longer. It would be an ordinary radio transmitter. Even radio waves "only" travel at the speed of light, and they can't go from one world to another.

THE SLOWNESS OF LIGHT

You might think that when you talk to someone on the telephone, or use the Internet, the communication happens instantly. But it doesn't. None of these everyday communications travels faster than light. It's just that the speed of light is so enormous. The distance from London to New York is about 3,500 miles. The speed of light is about 186,000 miles a second. So it takes ordinary communications like radio only 0.019 of a second to cross the Atlantic. That's just too quick for us to notice the delay.

If you were on the Moon, though, you would notice the delay. The Moon is 250,000 miles from Earth, so if you said "hello" into the radio transmitter in your spaceship, it would take about 1.3 seconds for the word to reach Earth. If ground control said "hello" straight back to you, it would take another 1.3 seconds to get to you.

So the gap between you saying hello and you hearing them say hello would be 2.6 seconds! It would make conversation pretty difficult.

But the lodestone resonator in the story isn't like that. As the Gallivespian spy Tialys has explained to Lyra, it communicates instantly across the worlds with its other half, with no delay at all, no matter how far apart the two halves of the resonator are. It certainly sounds magical. And yet, quantum entanglement is real science. It's the science that might explain the synchronicities that fascinated Carl Gustav Jung.

NEVER APART

Entanglement means that in the quantum world, once two things have interacted, they are always aware of what is happening to each other. Even if they are far apart, they behave as if they are joined together. It is as if they are never apart.

Remember that things like electrons aren't just particles in the everyday sense. They have a waviness associated with them too. Entanglement is when the waves of two quantum things get mixed up—tangled. Even if you move the "particles" far away from one another, so the waves are stretched out very thin, their tangled waves still send messages between the two particles.

The really amazing thing is that these messages take no time at all to travel between the particles. If two electrons got entangled, even if they moved so far apart that they were on opposite sides of the Galaxy, 100,000 light-years apart, if you poked one electron, the other one would jump. But if you wanted to see the other electron jump, you would have to wait 100,000 light-years for the light from it to travel across the Galaxy to you.

There is something else in the story that behaves like this: the angels Baruch and Balthamos. They love each other so deeply that even when they are far apart, each knows how the other one feels. And when Baruch is killed:

Balthamos felt the death of Baruch the moment it happened. He cried aloud and soared into the night air over the tundra, flailing his wings and sobbing his anguish into the clouds.

Lovers really do feel things like this, even when they are far apart. So do identical twins. That makes sense, because identical twins start their lives as a single egg cell that splits in two. You can't get much more entangled than that!

Science can't yet explain exactly what is going on when lovers and twins know things about their partners, even when the partners are far away. It still seems like magic to us, just like the planets moving around the Sun seemed like magic hundreds of years ago. But it might have something to do with quantum entanglement.

Riding on Light

Scientists don't understand exactly what goes on when twins and lovers are entangled, because they can't really do experiments on them. You can't very well kill somebody just to find out if their twin notices! But scientists can do experiments on quantum things, things like electrons, and the experiments prove that entanglement is real.

Lots of these experiments are done with

particles of light called photons. Earlier, we talked about light being a wave. But all quantum things are a mixture of wave and particle. In the same way that an electron is both a particle and a wave, light is both a wave and a particle. All quantum things have this dual nature.

One way to think of wave-particle duality is like a surfer riding a wave. The surfer can't get anywhere without the wave to ride on. Electrons ride on electron waves, and photons ride on light waves. But the waves are everywhere, and the particle "knows" what is happening to its wave anywhere in the Universe. So photons can become entangled, and even though they are made of light, messages between the tangled photons travel faster than light.

THE PROOF IN THE PUDDING

Very many experiments have been done that show entanglement works. The details are incredibly complicated (it's the sort of thing people win Nobel Prizes for), but it is easy to explain the principles of these experiments. You have to make an atom spit out two particles in opposite directions. Quantum physics says the particles must be entangled, because they start out from the same place. They might be photons or they might be electrons: it doesn't matter. What does matter is that they have to have a special kind of pair of properties. They mustn't be exactly the same as each other, but the difference between them has to be in balance, in a sense. If we were talking about people, it would be as if one of them had to be left-handed, and the other one right-handed. Or one is a boy and one is a girl.

In the quantum world, the special property might be polarization. One photon might have to be horizontally polarized, while the other one must be vertically polarized. It doesn't matter which one is which, but they can't both be the same.

To understand what is going on, we can think of these properties as colors. In our imaginary version of the experiment (equivalent to the real experiments), one photon has to be red and the other one blue. But still—and this is the crucial point—it doesn't matter which one is which.

In this situation, the photons themselves don't "know" what color they are, at first. They are in what is called a superposition of states, like the famous cat in Schrödinger's thought experiment (Chapter Five). The wave function of a photon only collapses when it is measured. Until one of them is measured, they are each in an undecided state, not sure if they are blue or red. But the two tangled photons must have different colors. So the very instant that you look at one of them and discover that it is blue, the wave function of the other photon collapses, and it "becomes" red. This happens without anyone looking at the other photon at all.

In the real experiments, this has been done (actually using polarizations, not colors) across a room. It has been proved that entanglement works, just the way the quantum rules said it should. The experimenters tickle an atom with electric fields (what Lyra would call anbaromagnetic fields), in a special way so that it spits out two photons in different directions. These photons have to have different polarizations, but it doesn't matter which one is which.

No human being could react quickly enough to measure the photons as they fly along, but the experiments are run automatically by a computer. If the computer makes one photon go through a vertical slit (like the picket fence we talked about in Chapter Nine), it forces that photon to be vertically polarized. Instantly, the other photon on the other side of the experiment becomes horizontally polarized, without being forced to go through any slits at all.

If the computer makes the first photon go through a horizontal "arrow slit," the second photon instantly settles into a vertically polarized state. The automatic experiment does this thousands and thousands of times, and always the quantum rules are obeyed.

PUTTING ENTANGLEMENT TO WORK

These experiments were carried out back in the 1970s. In the twenty-first century, scientists have gotten much further. Now they are putting entanglement to work, and maybe before too long we really will have something like the Gallivespians' lodestone resonator.

In 2002, a team of scientists in Australia managed to shift an entire laser beam sideways by a distance of about a yard, using quantum entanglement. They had one lot of photons in a laser beam and another lot of photons in another laser beam, all tangled with each other. By poking the first laser beam in the right way, using electromagnetic fields, they made all the photons twitch, and this made all the photons in the second beam twitch. All the information in the billions of photons in the first beam was transferred instantly to the other beam. But this destroyed the first beam. It was exactly as if the first beam of photons had been teleported a yard sideways. It did so without crossing the gap in between, and it took no time at all to make the jump.

One way this new technique will be used in the future is to make superfast computers that can shift information around inside themselves in no time at all. A range of a yard or so would be fine for that. But it doesn't look very impressive compared with the range of the Chevalier Tialys's resonator:

The instrument looked like a short length of pencil made of dull gray-black stone, resting on a stand of wood, and the Chevalier swept a tiny bow like a violinist's across the end while he pressed his fingers at various points along the surface. The places weren't marked, so he seemed to be touching it at random, but from the intensity of his expression and the certain fluency of his movements, Lyra knew it was as skillful and demanding a process as her own reading of the alethiometer.

The message Tialys is playing is transmitted, instantly, to an entangled resonator, the other half of his lodestone, which isn't even in the same world. But even this doesn't look so far-fetched in the twenty-first century as it might have when Philip Pullman wrote those words in the 1990s.

THE VOODOO BOMB

This is all a bit like voodoo. In voodoo, sometimes a doll is made to represent a real person. The hair or fingernail clippings of that person are attached to the doll, and this is supposed to make the voodoo doll have power over the person it represents. Voodoo believers think that if they stick a pin in the doll, that person will be hurt.

That's just like the bomb the Consistorial Court sets off at Saint-Jean-les-Eaux to try to kill Lyra, who is far away in the World of the Dead. The bomb has a piece of Lyra's hair, stolen from Mrs. Coulter's locket, in it. Because the cut-off hairs in the bomb are entangled with their roots on Lyra's head, the bomb's force will reach her, wherever she is. It fails only because Will is warned in time to cut away the roots of that lock of hair and seal them into yet another world, just before the bomb goes off.

"We place the hair in the resonating chamber. You understand, each individual is unique, and the arrangement of genetic particles quite distinct.... Well, as soon as it's analyzed, the information is coded in a series of anbaric pulses and transferred to the aiming device. That locates the origin of the material, the hair, wherever she may be...."

"The force of the bomb is directed by means of the hair?"

"Yes. To each of the hairs from which these ones were cut. That's right."

"So when it's detonated, the child will be destroyed, wherever she is?"

There was a heavy indrawn breath from the scientist, and then a reluctant "Yes."

There isn't really a voodoo effect that makes your neck hurt if a pin is stuck in the neck of a doll that represents you. Or a voodoo bomb. But there really is a real quantum entanglement effect that can now be made to send influences across several miles, even if not yet between worlds.

THE FUTURE IS NOW

The future—a time when communication across long distances using quantum entanglement is possible—may already be with us. Even in the 1990s, experimenters in Geneva were able to demonstrate entanglement using photons more than six miles apart. They made the entangled photons more or less in the way we have described, then sent one of the photons on a journey using the ordinary fiber-optic cables of the Swiss telephone system to a lab six miles away, before making the first photon twitch. The second photon twitched in exactly the same way that quantum physics had predicted. You could say that, like the laser beam in the Australian experiment, the first photon had been teleported across a distance of six miles. But there isn't very much information in a single photon.

The Australian experiment teleported a lot of information a short distance. The Swiss experiment teleported a little bit of information a long way. The latest experiments teleport a middling amount of information over middling distances—a couple of miles.

A BIT OF INFORMATION

Computer information is measured in bits. A "bit" of information is like a single switch that can be up or down, on or off. Each switch can either represent 0 (off) or 1 (on). These are the only two symbols in the binary code used by computers, but different strings of 0s and 1s can represent any number, or any letter of the alphabet, in binary code.

Eight bits of information make one byte. Because computers use binary code, on or off, we don't actually measure bytes in thousands and tens of thousands. Instead of measuring in tens, hundreds, thousands, and so on, in binary we measure in twos, fours, eights, and so on. In base ten (the way we usually count), the steps up the scale are counted by multiplying over and over again by ten: 10, 100, 1,000, and so on. The steps up the binary scale are actually counted by doubling the numbers over and over again: 2, 4, 8, 16, 32, 64, 128, 256, 512, 1,024, and so on. So 1,024 (2 multiplied by 2 nine times) is a natural unit in binary arithmetic, just as 1,000 (10 multiplied by 10 twice) is a natural unit in base ten arithmetic. This number, 1,024 bytes, is called a kilobyte, because it is roughly a thousand bytes, and we are used to counting in base ten. The same language is used for bigger numbers. The memory in the computer we are using to write this book has a capacity of 1 gigabyte, which is 1,024 megabytes, and each megabyte is 1,024 kilobytes. If you could make a system of entangled photons that involved a laser beam carrying a gigabyte of information, you could move all the information in our computer from one place to another, instantly.

Because they are working in the quantum world, the people who teleport photons call the bits of information they are working with qubits. This is short for quantum bit and is pronounced "cubit." A single photon could be either polarized vertically or polarized horizontally, representing 0 or 1 in the binary code. It can carry one qubit of data. A qubit is a bit of information stored in a photon, or in a single atom, or some other quantum entity. So far, the experimenters have only teleported a few qubits at a time using quantum entanglement. But at least it's a start.

These experiments were also carried out in Switzerland, at the end of 2002. The qubits stored on photons in one laboratory were transported by quantum entanglement onto photons in another laboratory 60 yards away. But although the two labs were so close, the connection between them was actually through a coil of optical fibers that would have stretched for over a mile if it had been unrolled. So we can already send a few qubits of information, instantly, across a distance of a mile, as if the space between the two ends of the cable did not exist. If scientists could do this without using the cable, they would have the beginnings of a communicator like the Gallivespians' lodestone resonator. And all because of entanglement.

Lyra & Will

If you think about it, the entire *His Dark Materials* story is about entanglement. There are lots of things in the story that are broken apart and failing, and Will and Lyra put them back together again. Things like the ghosts of the dead, who have been cut off from the living worlds and are freed so that their components can mingle with living material once again and become part of everything that is alive. Or the holes in space made by the windows that have been cut with the subtle knife, which Will teaches the angels to close up once again, as if healing the wounds.

And lots of the characters are entangled with one another. Not just Balthamos and Baruch, but Serafina Pekkala and Lee Scoresby, or Will's father and the witch Juta Kamainen, or even Lord Asriel and Mrs. Coulter. In Lyra's world, people are entangled with their dæmons. But most of all, Lyra is entangled with Will, and Will is entangled with Lyra.

At the end of the story, before Lyra and Will have to part forever, each to stay in their own world, Lyra shows Will a bench in the Botanic Garden in his Oxford, a bench that sits on the exact same spot as a bench in her world. They vow to return, each in their own world, to this exact spot every year at noon on Midsummer's Day, and sit for an hour, and know that the other is sitting in the same spot in their world. And after Lyra has returned to her own world forever, and Will has closed the last window between his world and hers and broken the subtle knife, she sits on the bench in her world, and wonders. Wonders:

... whether there would ever come an hour in her life when she didn't think of him—didn't speak to him in her head, didn't relive every moment they'd been together, didn't long for his voice and his hands and his love. She had never dreamed of what it would feel like to love someone so much; of all the things that had astonished her in her adventures, that was what astonished her the most. She thought the tenderness it left in her heart was like a bruise that would never go away, but she would cherish it forever.

Entanglement.

OTHER BOOKS
TO READ

✦

Gribbin, John. *Quantum Physics*. New York: Dorling Kindersley, 2002.

Gribbin, John. *Stardust*. New Haven, CT: Yale University Press, 2001.

Gribbin, Mary and John. *Chaos and Uncertainty*. London: Trafalgar Square Books, 1999.

Gribbin, Mary and John. *Eyewitness: Time & Space*. New York: Dorling Kindersley, 1998.

Hyde, Maggie, and Michael McGuiness. *Introducing Jung*. New York: National Book Network, 2001.

Roberts, Keith. *Pavane*. New York: Del Rey, 2001.

If you want to try something more advanced about quantum physics, see two other books by John Gribbin:

In Search of Schrödinger's Cat. New York: Bantam, 1984.

Schrödinger's Kittens and the Search for Reality. Boston: Back Bay, 1996.

GLOSSARY

atoms The building blocks from which all material objects in our world are made.

Aurora Another name for the Northern or Southern Lights.

baryonic matter Matter made up of atoms and molecules.

Big Bang The event in which our Universe was born, nearly 14 billion years ago.

binary code A code using only two symbols. Morse code is a binary code, and so is the code used in computers.

bit The smallest possible piece of information, equivalent to on/off or yes/no.

Butterfly Effect When a small change in initial conditions makes a big difference in where you end up.

byte Eight bits. A byte is like a word in the two-letter alphabet of binary code.

calcite Another name for Iceland spar.

chaos In science, the situation that occurs when the Butterfly Effect takes place.

charge See *electricity*.

Cold Dark Matter Matter that has never been seen but that astronomers know is there because of the way its gravity affects stars and galaxies.

Cosmos Another word for the Universe.

decay Another word for radioactivity.

electricity A property like magnetism that makes some particles, such as electrons, charged. Charged particles are influenced by magnetic fields.

electromagnetism The combination of magnetism and electricity.

electrons Fundamental, negatively charged particles that are components of atoms.

elements The simplest substances known. Each element is made of a single kind of atom.

entanglement In quantum physics, when two

things are aware of each other even when
they are far apart. Entanglement may explain
synchronicity.

Expanding Universe Another name for the Cosmos.
Our Universe is getting bigger as time
passes.

feedback When something that happens affects
itself.

Freudian slip A slip of the tongue that shows what
you are really thinking.

Gaia Name for the whole of our living planet,
from the name of the Greek goddess of
the Earth.

galaxy An island of stars in space. A single galaxy
may contain hundreds of billions of stars.

gravity The force that holds everything in the
Universe together. It also holds us down on
the surface of the Earth.

half-life The amount of time it takes for half of
the atoms in a piece of radioactive matter
to decay.

Iceland spar A natural crystal that acts like a prism
but splits light up in a curious way.

<u>I Ching</u> A kind of oracle originally used in China.

initial conditions Where something starts from.

ion An atom that has lost some of its electrons.

irrational numbers Numbers that cannot be written down as a ratio of two whole numbers.

lodestone An old name for magnetic pieces of rock.

magnetic field The region around a magnetic object (such as a lodestone) where a compass needle feels the influence of the magnetism.

magnetism The force that makes a compass needle point in a certain direction.

magnetosphere Another name for the region around the Earth where the magnetic field is strong.

molecules More-complicated building blocks than atoms, made up from atoms joined together in certain combinations.

natural selection The way evolution works by weeding out individuals that are not good at surviving.

neutrons Fundamental, electrically neutral particles that are components of atoms.

nucleus The central part of an atom.

oracle A holy person or place where people sought wisdom in ancient times.

parallel worlds Worlds that exist in their own dimensions of space and time, alongside our own Universe.

photon A particle of light, like a little burst of electromagnetic waves.

polarization A property of light that results from its waviness.

prism A triangle of glass used to make a spectrum.

protons Fundamental, positively charged particles that are components of atoms.

quantum physics The rules that describe the behavior of atoms and subatomic particles.

qubit A quantum bit, where one bit of information is stored in a form where the rules of quantum physics apply.

radioactivity When an atom spits out a particle and turns into an atom of a different element. Also called radioactive decay or decay.

serendipity When something nice happens by chance.

Solar System Our Sun and its family of planets, including the Earth and other objects.

Solar Wind A stream of particles (ions and electrons) that blows out from the Sun past the Earth.

space-time The dimensions that make up our Universe—three of space and one of time.

spectrum The pattern of colored light made when sunlight or starlight passes through a glass triangle or when sunlight is reflected through raindrops.

strings In quantum physics, the name given to little loops of stuff that vibrate inside particles.

subatomic particles The particles that make up an atom, including protons, neutrons, and electrons.

symbionts The living things involved in symbiosis.

symbiosis When two or more living things depend on each other for survival.

synchronicity When two things that seem to

happen by accident turn out to be
connected to one another.

Universe Everything that there is, including all
the stars, galaxies, and dark matter.

wave A ripple, like that on a pond; light and
radio waves are ripples of electromagnetism.

wave-particle duality In quantum physics, a theory
that holds that things like photons and
electrons behave sometimes like waves and
sometimes like particles.

Index

accelerators, 22

atoms, 5–11, 13, 23–24, 39–45, 73, 74

Index